Peter Birch Y6

2004 POETRY CO...

ONCE UPON A RHYME

IMAGINATION FOR A NEW GENERATION

South West England
Edited by Donna Samworth

First published in Great Britain in 2004 by:
Young Writers
Remus House
Coltsfoot Drive
Peterborough
PE2 9JX
Telephone: 01733 890066
Website: www.youngwriters.co.uk

All Rights Reserved

© *Copyright Contributors 2004*

SB ISBN 1 84460 582 5

Foreword

Young Writers was established in 1991 and has been passionately devoted to the promotion of reading and writing in children and young adults ever since. The quest continues today. Young Writers remains as committed to engendering the fostering of burgeoning poetic and literary talent as ever.

This year's Young Writers competition has proven as vibrant and dynamic as ever and we are delighted to present a showcase of the best poetry from across the UK. Each poem has been carefully selected from a wealth of *Once Upon A Rhyme* entries before ultimately being published in this, our twelfth primary school poetry series.

Once again, we have been supremely impressed by the overall high quality of the entries we have received. The imagination, energy and creativity which has gone into each young writer's entry made choosing the best poems a challenging and often difficult but ultimately hugely rewarding task - the general high standard of the work submitted amply vindicating this opportunity to bring their poetry to a larger appreciative audience.

We sincerely hope you are pleased with our final selection and that you will enjoy *Once Upon A Rhyme South West England* for many years to come.

Contents

Bridge Farm Junior School, Whitchurch
Rebecca Trotman (9)	1
Bethany Sparks (8)	1
Harriet Saunders (9)	2
Lauren Underhill (9)	2
Amy Long (8)	3
Carly Marsh (8)	3
Claire Saunders (9)	4
Connor Bressington (9)	4
Shannon Barkshire (9)	4
Francesca Smith (9)	5
Rebecca Whitehead (8)	5
Chloe Glenn (9)	5
James Shears-Browning (8)	6
James Russell (9)	6
Luke Mullins (8)	6
Gabriella Penny (9)	7

Clandown CE Primary School, Radstock
Danielle Hall (11)	7
Peter Helmore (11)	7
Michael Shave (11)	8
George Lock (11)	8
Chantelle Parsons (7)	9
Harry Lock (8)	9
Katie Jones (8)	9
Ethan Cooke (9)	10
Josh Cormack (8)	10
Michaela Gould (11)	11

Drybrook School, Drybrook
Lily Burford (9)	11
Abigail Greaves (8)	12
Alex Hetenyi (8)	12
Esme Ford (8)	13
Rebecca Hardy (9)	13
Georgina Brain (9)	14
Chloe A Matthews (9)	14

Marina Weaver (7)	15
Beth Grail (9)	15
Rachel Wilks (8)	16
Abby Hughes (9)	16
Tom James (9)	17
Jim Rushworth (9)	17
Jake Atrill (8)	18
Thomas Leadbeater (7)	18
Tom Burford (8)	19

Flax Bourton CE VC Primary School, Bristol

Sebastian Bartlett (11)	19
Ryan Collins (10)	20
James Michallat (10)	20
Mitchell Spencer (10)	21
Ashley Crossey (10)	21
Scott Davies (10)	22
Tyler O'Brien (10)	22
Sian Eilish Cogan (11)	22
Olivia Smith (11)	23

Hopelands School, Stonehouse

Jessica McGill (11)	23

Huish Episcopi Primary School, Langport

Jamie Douglas & Amiee Stone (10)	24
Holly Fraser & Lucy Cox (9)	24
Lily Coker (10)	24
Kieron Brain (9)	25
Abbie Martin (9)	25
Katie Forrester (9)	26
Yasmin Webb (9)	26
Edward Coate (9)	27
Linden Derham (9)	27
Louis Jenkinson (9)	28
Michael Cox (9)	28
Jade Beer (8)	28
Alice Bown (9)	29
Hannah Harris (9)	29
Jasmine Stott (9)	29
Charlie Keywood (8)	30

Gregory Watson (9) 30
Sinead Shephard (9) 31
Steven Langford (9) 31
Matthew Joyner (9) 32
Kayleigh Scadden (9) 32
Abbie Bown (10) 32
Belinda Massmann-Oakley (10) 33
Cara Sedgwick (9) 33
Sophie Palmer (9) 34

Iron Acton CE Primary School, Bristol
Hannah Lloyd (9) 34
Alex Ashford (9) 35
Ioni Bellis (9) 36
Emma Pilgrim (10) 36
Richard Wiggins (10) 37
Rosie Brindle (10) 37
Rebecca Barlow (10) 38
Alistair Mansfield (10) 38
Hannah Byrne (9) 39
Devon Kimberley (9) 39
Sadie Perks (8) 40

Longborough CE Primary School, Moreton-In-Marsh
Chris Appleton (10) 40
Emma Cook (8) 41
Rachel Deane (9) 41
Lily Willcocks (10) 42
Alex Dewhurst (10) 42
Nathan Long (10) 43
Samuel Mazur (11) 43
Ted Turvey (11) 44
Amber Griffin (11) 44
Jade Temple (10) 44
Kyle Ellery (11) 45

Lovington CE VC Primary School, Somerset
George Stuckey (10) 45
Emma Simmonds (11) 46
Ben Talbot (10) 46
Oliver Veryard (10) 47

Tom Tubridy (10)	47
Jade Glover (11)	48
Kane Clarke (11)	49
Amanda Matthews (10)	49
Jake Witherington (11)	50
Libby Graham (10)	50
Harriet Ffooks (10)	51
Tommy Reynolds (9)	51
Stephanie Thayer (10)	52

Mitton Manor Primary School, Tewkesbury

Eleanor Kelly (10)	52
Annie Wilkinson (10)	53
Wayne Greening (9)	53
Chloe Mason (10)	54
Elena Amadeo (9)	54
Jessica Perry (9)	55
Elly King (9)	55
Roseanna Davis (10)	56
Kiera Newborough (10)	56
Jessica Bouwer (9)	57
Lauren Grainger (10)	57
Lizzie Clarke (10)	58
Ben Carter (10)	58
Tom Allcoat (10)	59
Sam Gaisford (10)	59
Helen Thompson (9)	60
Samantha Danter (10)	61
Katherine Nash (9)	61
Ellen Kettell (9)	62
Sam Rayner (10)	63
Owen Vincent (9)	64
Baptiste Nottingham (10)	64
Oliver Francis (9)	65
Emma Williams (10)	65
Tom Lewis (10)	66
Sam Gray (10)	66
Laura Griffin (10)	67

Pauntley CE Primary School, Newent
Tasmin Jones (10) 67
Danielle Trevail (11) 68
Luke Hodgin (11) 69

Pendock CE Primary School, Pendock
Josh Hunt 69
Emma Mealing   (9) 70
Jade Taylor 70
Katie Leigh 71
Isobel Williams (8) 71
Rhiannon King (7) 72
Ryan Keyte (9) 72
Thomas Jones 73
Chloe Darrell 73
Holly Neal (8) 74
Kiya Hughes 74
Jordan-Marie Welsh 75
Sophie Eggerton 75
Cameron Dallimore 76

Perry Court Junior School, Hengrove
Katherine Voysey (11) 76
Joshua Vowles (9) 77
Jordan Edwards (10) 77
Jordan Davies (11) 78
Colby Avent (9) 78
Max Pearce (10) 78
Emily Butler (11) 79
Sophie Higgins, Kayla Whippey & Natalie Wookey (10) 79
Aaron Meredith (11) 79
Lucy Hacker (11) 80
Emily Brown (11) 80
Kayleigh Clark, Paige Tripp-Edwards, Leah Fisher (10) 81
James Perry & Jacob Pocock (10) 81
Carly Thomas (11) 82

St John's Catholic Primary School, Bath
Sophia Mulvihill (8) 82
Tom Morris (10) 83

Steven Pearce (8)	83
Sophie Teasdale (8)	83
Phoebe Langley (10)	84
Anna Piercy (11)	84
Alice Piekarski (10)	85
Camilla Bartolo (10)	85
Christian Preston (9)	85
Joshua Walker (11)	86
Kristian Morrison (10)	86
Conor Sheridan (8)	86
Alice May (10)	87
Joseph Marchant (11)	87
Amy Morris (10)	88
Tess Henderson (10)	88
Ryan Farrington (10)	89
Emily Burford (8)	89
Charlie Francis (9)	89
Tess O'Hara (9)	89
Callum Stevenson (9)	90
Sophie Southcott (9)	90
Beatrice Moody (9)	90
Charlotte Dixon (9)	90
Olivia Coles (9)	91
Joshua Ayres (10)	91
Amy Donohue (8)	91
Alex Keitch (10)	92
Sam Morris (8)	92
Hannah Phillips (10)	92
Emer Heatley (9)	93
Tom Prangley (11)	93
Amelia Morris Cuthbertson (8)	93
Laura King (10)	94
Lauren Tucker (10)	94
Daniel Malinowski (9)	94
Joseph Roberts (11)	95
Olivia Farrington (7)	95
Louis Mancini (8)	95
Alessandra Di Vincenzo (8)	95
James Piercy (8)	96
Talent Gwekwerere (11)	96
Emma Scolding (9)	97
Ciara Hughes (7)	97

Tom Langley (8)	97
Jack Sherry (9)	98
Maria Kelleher (8)	98
Victoria Prangley (7)	98
India Jaggon-Barrett	99
George Cox (10)	99
Rebecca Harding (8)	99
Emily Kelson (9)	100
Ellie Bassett (9)	100
Jack Chalmers (10)	101
Eleanor Parker (10)	101
Grace McPherson (9)	102
Rowland Goodbody (11)	102
Stefanie Gomez-Lugue (11)	103
Gwyn West (9)	103
Benedict King (9)	104
Matteo Sunda (10)	104
Elizabeth Richardson (8)	105
Thomas Johnson (10)	105
Mary Etheridge (8)	105
Hannah May (9)	106

St Joseph's Catholic Primary School, Fishponds

Katie McCarthy (10)	106
Samantha Haggett (10)	107
Sammi Hollis (11)	107
Amy Adlard (10)	108
Terry Woodmen Smart (10)	108
Amardeep Sahota (11)	109
Jordan Silk (11)	109
Helen Smith (10)	110
Georgina Ford (11)	110
Alicia Chilcott (11)	111
Emily White (10)	111
Alex McKeigue (11)	112
Abby O'Brien (10)	112
Megan Price (11)	113
Daniel Cook (11)	113
Jordan Carey (10)	114
Jack Kilbane (11)	114
Claire Anne O'Mahony (11)	115

Yolanda Downer (10)	115
Almaz Larkin Williams (11)	116
Samantha Lee (11)	116
Zoe Davis (11)	117

St Lawrence CE Primary School, Lechlade

Remy Chaplais (10) & Sam Taylor (11)	117
James Russell (10)	118
Luke Hewens (10)	119
Alicia Gear (10)	119
Jack Lea (11)	120
Clare Hirons (11)	120
Simon Booth (11)	121
Rachael Ashard (11)	121
Jay Goddard (11)	122
Patrick Docker & Ashley Bennett (10)	122
Ellie Popp (11)	123
Thomas Jenkins (11)	123
Oliver Codling (11)	124
Camilla Hewens (10)	125
Kimberley Bloomer (11)	125

St Mary's CE VC Primary School, Bridport

Amelia Tucker (10)	126
Hannah Willoughby (9)	126
Bianca Harp (9)	127
Daniel Dew (9)	127
Lizzy Perry (9)	128
Jamie Riggs (9)	128
Vanessa Thurston (9)	129
Ashley Lewis (9)	129
Charlie Lawrence (9)	130
Stephanie Aburrow (10)	130
Tessa Summerfield (10)	131
Boris Hanrahan-Lane (10)	131

St Mary's CE VA Primary School, Thornbury

Katherine Gardner (8)	132
Lydia Rygol (8)	132
Hannah Turvey (8)	133

Arran Riordan (8)	133
Henry Wilmer & Zara Crocker (7)	134

Sharpness Primary School, Berkeley

Ashleigh Heeps (9)	135
Henry Knight (9)	136
Jacob Wedgbury (9)	137
Daniel Brown (8)	138
Joshua Crew (9)	138
Michael Turl (8)	139
Matthew Turl (8)	139

Silverhill School, Winterbourne

Charlotte Low (9)	140
Jasmine Ayres (9)	140
Ben Mountain (11)	140
Abbie Scott (9)	141
Shannon Webb (8)	141
Ella Brown (9)	141
Perry Williams (10)	142
Cameron Nixon (9)	142
Nicola Bibb (8)	143
Hayley Taylor (9)	143
Jamie Floyd (8)	143
Kate Brown (8)	144
Ben Carter (9)	144
Bryony Wintle (9)	144
Emma Strangward-Pryce (11)	145
Tom Croucher (10)	145
Ellie Stephens (10)	146
George Mills-Gerrard (8)	146
Annabelle Goddard (10)	147
Ben Brown (9)	147
Jodie Turner (9)	148
Tom Frost (10)	148
Chloe Brown (9)	148
Jack Williams (8)	149
Kerry Davies (11)	149
Sarah Bradley (10)	150
Olivia Stewart (8)	150
Annabel Mills (10)	151

Anna-Marie Connolly (8)	151
Adam Hay (11)	152
Gabriella Chaplin (9)	152
Daniel Perry (9)	153
Elliott Giles (10)	153
Gemma Childs (10)	154
Andrew Pagett (11)	154
Peter Hodges (10)	155
Zak Milsom (11)	155
Zoë Hughes (11)	156
Dan Coley (10)	156
Chelsie Sparks (8)	157
Sophie Bruce (10)	157
Mairead Connolly (11)	158
Rosanna Tregear (10)	159
George Williams (10)	159
Hannah Cooke (8)	159
Ross Lee (11)	160
Holly Parfitt (10)	160
Charles Fisher (7)	161

Southill Primary School, Weymouth

Rebecca Andrews (10)	161
Elouise Langton (10)	161
Rhys Diplock (10)	162
Chelsie Narraway-Syme (10)	162
Samuel	162
Ross Johnson (10)	163
Michael James (9)	163
Matthew Owen (10)	163
Natasha Hazell (9)	164
Jodie Symes (10)	164
Keeley Filmer (9)	164
Nathan Osmond (10)	164
Charlotte Millar (10)	165
Irina Burnet (10)	165
Emily Filmer (10)	165
Hannah Pullen (10)	166
Olivia Walker (10)	166
Toby Mason (9)	166
Farron Aitken (9)	167

Nicola Sharpe (10)	167
Jak Terrell (10)	167

SS Peter & Paul Primary School, Redland

Sebastian Appleby (8)	168
Francesca Orlando (8)	168
Christian Holland (8)	169
Ben Murphy (8)	169
Lewis Cunningham (9)	170
Adel Mebarek (7)	170
Leonora Hamilton-Shield (8)	170
Marino Olivieri (8)	171
Brendan Perkins (10)	171
Ben Gompels (8)	172
Noah Begbie-Crewe (8)	172
Myfanwy Rothery (10)	172
Wilf de Salis (8)	173
Melanie Ginestier (8)	173
Zaid Ahsan (10)	174
Marco Olivieri (10)	174
Emmanuelle Ginestier (10)	174
Peter Birch (10)	175
Jessie de Salis (10)	175
Martha Dooley (9)	176
Ben Mitchell (10)	176
Olivia Lang (8)	176
Matthew Gompels (9)	177
Ceni Owen (10)	177
Connor Murphy (10)	177
Sally Sterling (10)	178
Zoe Rice (10)	178
Edward Lang (10)	178
Sam Mason (8)	179
Patrick Burke (8)	179
Julien Harrison (9)	179
Louise Caldwell (9)	180
Ellie Craig (10)	180
Eva Mason (10)	181
Jacqueline Roy (11)	181
Laura Vaughan (10)	182

Steam Mills Primary School, Cinderford

Bethany Hopkins (10)	182
Craig White (10)	183
Luke Haddon (10)	183
Aimee Fennell (10)	183
Stephen Penn (11)	184
Jordan Niblett (10)	184
Matthew Jones (11)	185
Callum Marsh (11)	185
Jessica Hale (10)	186
Wesley Davis-James (10)	186
Shantelle Minchin (12)	186
Joy Fellows (11)	187
Alex Powell (10)	187
Izzie Gazzard	187
Fiona Wicks (10)	188
Jack Freeman (9)	188
Chelsea Meek (10)	188
Jade Burford (11)	189
Joseph Freeman (11)	189
Olivia Pritchard (10)	189
Gemma Taylor (11)	190

Tatworth Primary School, Chard

Kieran Powell (10)	190
Charlie Carter (11)	190
Joe Hare (11)	191
Nathan Borthwick (10)	191
Nick Mouland (10)	191
Beth Lewis (10)	192
Kayleigh White (11)	192
Freddie Henry (10)	193
Henry Morgan (11)	193
Kelly Taylor (11)	194
Peter Jeanes (11)	194
Ben Mear (10)	194
Charles Allen-Roberts (11)	194
Christopher Hodder (11)	195

Twigworth CE Primary School, Twigworth
    Celine Parsons (8)   195
    Kelly de Vos (7)   195
    Sheraleen Crocker   195
    Charlotte Burrowes (7)   196
    Nelson Royles   196
    Georgia Phillips (9)   196
    Jordan Watts & Oliver Brown   196

Winsham Primary School, Winsham
    Mervyn Webster (8)   197
    Kieran Bailey (9)   197
    Louise Johnson (10)   197
    Samuel Harris (9)   198
    Michael Pugh (9)   198
    Benjamin Harris (11)   198
    Billie-Ann Warren (11)   199
    Cain Davies (8)   199
    Adrian Shakespeare (9)   199
    Kirsty Love (9)   200
    Scott Curtis (10)   200

The Poems

Through That Door

Through that door,
Is a deep blue sea,
Where dolphins play,
And fishes swim.
On the seabed
Octopuses crawl,
And crabs move sideways
Where turtles swim
And fishes dart
With their tiny fins flapping
The stingray slowly
Sliding across the sand
Waiting for its prey.
And seaweed gently sways
Waving at the passers going by
The anemone
Where clownfish live
With their black and white stripes
And the big blue whale swims past
As slowly as a snail.

Rebecca Trotman (9)
Bridge Farm Junior School, Whitchurch

Through That Door

Through that door
Is an enchanted jungle
Where cheetahs run
And monkeys swing
Where 10 metres down
In a dark place
There lies a pit of dead animal bones
And the finest fur.

Bethany Sparks (8)
Bridge Farm Junior School, Whitchurch

Through That Door

Through that door
Is a mysterious school,
Where ghosts glide
And the classrooms
As cold as snow
A wizard who
Can't predict magic
And the teachers have
All turned to bones
Their hall is nearly half
The size of the school
With hundreds or chairs
And four huge tables,
Down in the chamber lies Fluffy
The three-headed dog
Through that door
Everyone's *dead!*

Harriet Saunders (9)
Bridge Farm Junior School, Whitchurch

I'm Inside Looking Outside

I'm inside looking outside at the falling rain
I'm outside looking inside at the windowpane
I'm inside looking outside at the dazzling sun
I'm outside looking inside at the hot cross bun
I'm inside looking outside, hey can you see that ship?
I'm outside looking inside at the small round pip
I'm inside looking outside at the pencil case
I'm outside looking inside at the ugly face
I'm inside looking outside at a yellow room
I'm outside looking inside at a very high moon.

Lauren Underhill (9)
Bridge Farm Junior School, Whitchurch

Through That Door

Through that door
Is countryside
Where reflections are in the water with nobody there
And shadows on the floor.
Then a ghost appeared to scare me out of my skin
                                  and all that's left is my bones.

Through that door
Is Dinosaur land
Where T-rexs prowl
And diplodocus groan
And then the T-rex came and chased me

Through that door
Is a fairyland
With fairies covered in glitter
With wands like lightning
And toadstools like spotty sweets on sticks.

Through that door
Is a dungeon
With skeletons with chains on their wrists
Some were being hung by the neck with a long rope
The purest bones and coins were scattered on the floor.

Amy Long (8)
Bridge Farm Junior School, Whitchurch

I'm Inside Looking Outside

I'm inside looking outside at the darling sun
I'm outside looking inside at the hot cross bun
I'm inside looking outside; hey can you see that ship?
I'm outside looking inside at the small round pip
I'm inside looking outside at that aeroplane
I'm outside looking inside; hey can you see that toy crane?

Carly Marsh (8)
Bridge Farm Junior School, Whitchurch

Through That Door

Through that door is a long and extremely tall cliff
Where a little girl and her teddy are sat on the white edge
And as she was gently sat with her white gown soon to be black
She turned around to look at the dark blue door
                                      and said a soft goodbye
I wonder why she said goodbye
It sounds like she was mistreated but it's too late
I can't ask her now
It's too late.

Claire Saunders (9)
Bridge Farm Junior School, Whitchurch

Through That Door

Through that door
Is an enchanted wood
Where magic elves sing
And green goblins skip,
Where foals prance
And Pinocchio dances
Where dragons fly
And magic magicians cry.

Connor Bressington (9)
Bridge Farm Junior School, Whitchurch

I'm Inside Looking Outside

I'm inside looking outside at the falling rain
I'm outside looking inside through the windowpane
I'm outside looking inside at the yellow room
I'm inside looking outside at the dazzling moon.

Shannon Barkshire (9)
Bridge Farm Junior School, Whitchurch

I'm Inside Looking Outside

I'm inside looking outside at the glowing sun
I'm outside looking inside at the hot yummy bun
I'm inside looking outside listening to the birds chirping
I'm outside looking inside at the stove cooking
I'm inside looking outside at the falling snow
I'm outside looking inside at the fire glowing
I'm inside looking outside.

Francesca Smith (9)
Bridge Farm Junior School, Whitchurch

I'm Inside Looking Outside

I'm inside looking outside at the bold glazing sun
I'm outside looking inside I can see the rabbit's hut
I'm inside looking outside at the flying aeroplane
I'm looking outside at the blue sky
I'm looking outside at the lovely space of land
I'm looking outside at the joke man.

Rebecca Whitehead (8)
Bridge Farm Junior School, Whitchurch

I'm Inside Looking Outside

I'm inside looking outside at the glazing sun
I'm outside looking inside I can see the rabbits run
I'm looking inside at the flying aeroplane
I'm looking outside at the blue sky
But I'm inside at the lovely space of land
I'm looking outside at the joke man.

Chloe Glenn (9)
Bridge Farm Junior School, Whitchurch

I'm Inside Looking Outside

I'm inside looking outside at the big fat men
I'm outside looking inside at a wobbly can
I'm inside looking outside at the pouring rain
I'm inside looking outside watching the twisting tornado
I'm inside looking outside gazing up at the moon
I'm outside looking inside at a sizzling sausage
I'm inside looking outside watching a plane fly by.

James Shears-Browning (8)
Bridge Farm Junior School, Whitchurch

I'm Inside Looking Outside

I'm inside looking outside at the growing grass
I'm outside looking inside at the crystal glass
I'm inside looking outside at the birds singing
I'm outside looking inside listening to the phone ring
I'm inside looking outside at a bear
I'm outside looking inside at a wooden chair.

James Russell (9)
Bridge Farm Junior School, Whitchurch

I'm Inside Looking Outside

I'm inside looking outside at the growing grass
I'm outside looking inside at the crystal glass
I'm inside looking outside listening to the birds sing
I'm outside looking inside listening to the phone ring
I'm inside looking outside at a bear
I'm outside looking inside at a wooden chair.

Luke Mullins (8)
Bridge Farm Junior School, Whitchurch

I'm Inside Looking Outside

I'm inside looking outside at the dazzling sun
I'm outside looking inside at the bright lights of the room
I'm inside looking outside listening to the birds
I'm outside looking inside listening to the television.

Gabriella Penny (9)
Bridge Farm Junior School, Whitchurch

Blue Dolphin

B lue ballet dolphin swims,
L ush smooth water,
U nderwater to catch my prey,
E at it up in a great big gulp.

D ive down deeper and deeper,
O ceans open wide,
L aughter heard around the sea
P redators always looking for me
H iding myself to play hide-and-seek,
I am so intelligent
N ight is so peaceful for me and my friends.

Danielle Hall (11)
Clandown CE Primary School, Radstock

Sunset

S o bright that your eyes close up,
U nder from the water it comes
N early the end of the day,
S o we'll be back tomorrow,
E veryone is tired,
T he sun has gone.

Peter Helmore (11)
Clandown CE Primary School, Radstock

Dog

My pup Max is full of fun,
Listen to what he has done,
Makes mum mad at me,
I miss my tea!
Go to my room, then all you can
Hear is - boom! boom!
I live in fear.

Max is funny, small and loveable
Although capable of causing trouble.
Chewing up shoes,
Digging up the garden
Burying bones,
All the time he really knows . . .
Loveable, cuddly,
Max is mine.

Michael Shave (11)
Clandown CE Primary School, Radstock

Wizard's Staff

W icked wands with wonderful spells
 I n the night, horrific fright
Z any staff and super wands
A gainst the evil,
R eady to fight
D oing amazing spells
S uper power forced to you.

S laying his enemy
T aking the soul
A fter a battle
F ire of doom
F earsome force of evil.

George Lock (11)
Clandown CE Primary School, Radstock

Sunshine

S un is really hot
U nder you swim, sunshine
N obody was good at the beach!
S un was a bit hot for my baby sister, and me
H ot, and you put on some sun lotion,
I ce cream to make you feel better,
N ever go right out in the water
E veryone jumps in the blue cold water.

Chantelle Parsons (7)
Clandown CE Primary School, Radstock

The Cat Chase

Once a cat was scratching a leather sofa,
A dog came and chases the cat up the stairs,
The cat jumped out of the window and onto the conservatory roof,
He jumped again and landed on the ground
The dog went out the back door,
He started to chase the poor worn out cat round the garden
The dog was worn out too and gave up!

Harry Lock (8)
Clandown CE Primary School, Radstock

Holidays

H olidays are fun for everyone
O n the beach, it is really cool . . .
L ollies, ice-cold from the freezer
I ce cream, luscious for everyone
D ays are warm at the beach
A ll the holidaymakers are bright red and hot,
Y achts for people who like sailing
S and of fire on my soles!

Katie Jones (8)
Clandown CE Primary School, Radstock

Animals And Pets

A sheep fluffy,
N atterjack spotty,
I nsects creepy,
M ice squeaky
A nimals brilliant
L izards fast,
S nakes slithery.

A pes acrobatic
N arwals great,
D olphins intelligent

P andas friendly
E lephants big
T igers fierce
S corpions deadly.

Ethan Cooke (9)
Clandown CE Primary School, Radstock

Soccer Star

S core!
O pen goal,
C ommentator,
C hristian Roberts
E qualizer
R ed and white shirt

S occer,
T alented,
A ccurate scorer,
R ich.

Josh Cormack (8)
Clandown CE Primary School, Radstock

Seaside

S un bright yellow in the sky
E at your sandwiches on the sand
A t the sea the water is really cold
S eagulls are eating my chips!
I n the arcades it is really cool
D ad jumps in the water,
E veryone is soaking wet!

Michaela Gould (11)
Clandown CE Primary School, Radstock

Thunder

Thunder whirled and screeched,
As if it was coming back for revenge.
Thunder covered the sun,
And the world went dark like in a black and white movie.
Thunder swept around,
In a bad mood
Thunder slipped under cars,
Like it was controlling them.

Thunder whistled and wailed,
Around the murky sea.
Thunders creeping everywhere like a lost dog,
Then it drags across the sky
Like a pale grey ghost.
Roaring away the thunder screamed,
Like a grumpy baby.
Then the thunder slipped away,
Like a slinky cat.
Goodbye thunder

Lily Burford (9)
Drybrook School, Drybrook

The Ice

The ice raced across the ground
Like a glittering blanket spread out over the land,
It slept on the pond and the grass,
It hung down like long spindly fingers.

The ice was as white as a polar bear
As white as a piece of white paper,
Colder than anything on earth
Glittering like diamonds on the grass.

Slowly melting in the blazing sun
Like nothing ever happened disappearing,
Crying, crying because it was vanishing,
In the morning it has all gone.

Next winter reappearing on the ground,
Like glittering diamonds covering everything,
Waiting for the blazing sun to come out,
Making it vanish till next winter.

Abigail Greaves (8)
Drybrook School, Drybrook

Trees Through The Day

Leaves blew across the sky
Like a hawk swooping down, crossing the sky.

The wind blew and the trees bent down
As if they were bowing to the grass.

Leaves play peep-and-seek inside their bud
As the sun begins to grow.

As the tree looks up at his new born leaves
The darkness falls from the sky.

Alex Hetenyi (8)
Drybrook School, Drybrook

The Sea

As it chews the rocks
And rots the wood.

It swishes and sways,
Ripples into the beach
Rushes and crinkles
And slaps the rocks
Like a thousand hands.

Like a blue sky sharing
Secrets with the sea
Rushing and gushing
It explores the world.

Together they explore
Like a million tourists
Going around the world

They always meet new places
Like a thing that never ends.

Esme Ford (8)
Drybrook School, Drybrook

Daffodils

The daffodils sang at the sight of dawn
Like a flute playing.

The daffodils danced in the night
Like sparkling stars up in the midnight sky.

The daffodils laughed in the sunshine
Like children playing in the park.

The daffodils dreamed in silence
Like a TV on the mute

The daffodils cried when it rains
They cried like a hungry baby.

The daffodils played in the wind
As the wind pushed them side-to-side.

Rebecca Hardy (9)
Drybrook School, Drybrook

Thunder

The thunder drove all the gorgeous leaves off all the trees
Like shells getting swept away by a strong tide
Gulp, gulp
The thunder drank the last of the seas, rivers and streams
Like a thirsty giant gulping down its black coffee.
It laughed a sinister laugh
As loud as a lawnmower.

The thunder snarled and scratched
Like a savage guard dog
Trying to protect its owner from a murderer.
The thunder wailed
Like a ghost sent by the tortured dead
That had sworn revenge
The thunder cried, gasped and howled
The tone as low as a trumpet
As it faded away forever.

Georgina Brain (9)
Drybrook School, Drybrook

Wind

The wind came like a whisk spinning around the world.
The children stared as it raged about.
It slipped under the clouds and sun through the open air,
And hid between the trees.
Then gave a loud roar just like the thunder
Then he started to get very angry
 And moaned, then suddenly *kaboom!*
A great storm started
And everyone raced for shelter.

Chloe A Matthews (9)
Drybrook School, Drybrook

Daffodils

The morning had begun, a new autumn day
The daffodils danced and sang to the wind,
They swayed like a scarf in the breeze.

They knew it was getting near winter,
And they slept all winter long,
Like a baby in a cradle.

They dreamt and dreamt,
They dreamt they danced on the sun,
Like a ballerina dancing on a stage.

When spring came they awoke
And smiled at the butterflies flying past,
Like a paper aeroplane drifting by.

Marina Weaver (7)
Drybrook School, Drybrook

Thunder

The thunder danced around the sky.
It whistled like a child howling.

The thunder raged across the sky
It came like a sudden flash.

It feasted on the village below
Like a complaining little child.

The thunder drowned the sky.
It shook the floor as it passed.

The thunder forgot to roar
Like a clown forgetting to laugh.

Beth Grail (9)
Drybrook School, Drybrook

The Clouds

The clouds complained,
Like a brother or sister.

The clouds roared at the sky
Like your belly rumbling

The clouds sang
Like a harp playing

The clouds are
As soft as a feather.

The clouds have been crying,
Like a baby.

The clouds danced,
Like a paintbrush painting a canvas.

Rachel Wilks (8)
Drybrook School, Drybrook

The Wind

Dancing through the night like a ballerina
Pirouetting through the leaves,
Jumping and jiving through the trees.

The wind tiptoed through the dawn,
Over the hills, cross the lawns,
As if the clouds were giggling.

The wind clambered through the air,
Like a quick dart,
Doing mischief.

Abby Hughes (9)
Drybrook School, Drybrook

Daffodils

The daffodils moaned at the winter rain.
They glistened at the sight of dawn.

They ducked as the rain went past
They thought it was morning.

The daffodils smiled in the winter sunshine
Shaking the water from their leaves.

They laughed like a clown
Bouncing around a circus ring.

The daffodils danced like a ballerina
Swaying and floating in the wind.

They stood as still as stone
It seemed like summer.

The daffodils slept all autumn long.

Tom James (9)
Drybrook School, Drybrook

Trees

The snow painted the trees white
The birds started an enormous flight

The birds whispered with the clouds
Like a bird whistling proud.

The trees complained really loudly
Like an aeroplane soaring down.

The leaves blew across the sea
Like a seagull swooping low.

Jim Rushworth (9)
Drybrook School, Drybrook

Butterflies

Butterflies were as big as a cat
Safeguarding their pollen from bees,
Attacking caterpillars for food.

Gossiping butterflies drank their pollen,
Like a monster gulping blood,
Flying round like a tornado,
Like the wind covering the air.

Butterflies flew outside in the wilderness
Meeting other animals outside
Butterflies like an eagle flying fast as thunder
Chasing after his tiny rats.

Jake Atrill (8)
Drybrook School, Drybrook

Ice

Like a frozen solar field
Covered in Jack Frost's little present
As the blizzard raged up high
Like slippery ice cubes in the road
In the thick white snow
As a foul wind wipes the snow away
Like ice cubes raining down onto earth
That ice has taken over as everything gets
Wiped away all hope is lost as it fades
Like bits of diamond raining down
From above covered in snow from the
Sky it falls as the coldness races down.

Thomas Leadbeater (7)
Drybrook School, Drybrook

The Rain

The clouds rise
At sudden daylight
Like a storm cracking instantly

Painting the ground with puddles
As it bursts out like a dripping tap.

Soaking the children of the new day
Like a soggy towel wetter than anything.

Tom Burford (8)
Drybrook School, Drybrook

When The Tornado Came

Tornados spinning all around
Picking up children from
The ground people
Cleaning litter up
Tornados
Spreading it all
People orbiting
In the air, people
Are really scared
People are running
Everywhere, when
The tornado is in
The air, when the
Tornado is gone
Everybody
Goes outside
And says 'What
A horror'.

Sebastian Bartlett (11)
Flax Bourton CE VC Primary School, Bristol

Venus Is Orbiting The Sun

On Tuesday the 8th June
Venus is orbiting the sun
Oak class left their classroom
The eclipse we saw was fun.

The image we saw
From binoculars we wore
Was reflected on the floor
To stop our eyes from being sore.

The planet we say
Reflected on the floor
Looked as small as a mosquito
Sitting on a thorn.

Ryan Collins (10)
Flax Bourton CE VC Primary School, Bristol

Fantastic Football

F antastic football
O ut on the pitch
O wen shooting
T ipped over by the goalie for a corner
B eckham taking
A fantastic strike
L eroy Lita scoring
L ong live All Stars.

James Michallat (10)
Flax Bourton CE VC Primary School, Bristol

Sport

The football you watch
The rugby you play
How much fun are you having today?

I play with my friends
And we go to our dens
Until we box and that really rocks.

Basketball on a pitch
Golf on a course
Tennis on a court
I like all of the sport.

Mitchell Spencer (10)
Flax Bourton CE VC Primary School, Bristol

Summer Days!

The summer season is here
The pollen levels are high
And it's hot and stuffy in the sky.

The summer season is here
I doubt you will get a cold
That will make you feel extremely old.

The summer season is here
Autumn is next door,
And every leaf starts to fall to the floor.

Ashley Crossey (10)
Flax Bourton CE VC Primary School, Bristol

Life In The Jungle

Monkeys swinging in the vines
Like Tarzan swinging vine to vine
They scuttle up the trees like silly people,
The moss upon the giant trees,
Down come all the pretty leaves
Down and down they will not stop
Let's catch them all and play a lot.

Scott Davies (10)
Flax Bourton CE VC Primary School, Bristol

Sport Poem

Boxing on the TV
Football on the pitch
Pulling people over on a rugby ground
Gives me a stitch.

Tennis on a court
A caddy on a golf course
I am excited about to play basketball
And I love to ride a horse.

Tyler O'Brien (10)
Flax Bourton CE VC Primary School, Bristol

It's Me Against The World

It's me against the world
My heart is spinning
I don't know what's happening
I think the world is winning.

I feel a lot better
I don't know how
I've joined the world
I've joined it right now.

Sian Eilish Cogan (11)
Flax Bourton CE VC Primary School, Bristol

Seasons

Spring
Flowers springing in the air
Lots and lots everywhere
We are so glad spring has come
The flowers are so pretty I pick some.

Summer
The summer days are here
The blue sky is clear
The days are very bright
In the starry night

Autumn
The trees have lost their bright leaves
Now we must enjoy this season's trees
The trees have gone bare
So then they are left with nothing there

Winter
The winter days are very cold
And I feel like I am very old
We see a shooting star appear
I am very proud and dear

Then it comes to the end of the season
And becomes warm again.

Olivia Smith (11)
Flax Bourton CE VC Primary School, Bristol

Imaginary Friend

Here we go take a bow,
Because we're both over now,
There's a beginning and an end
But this is sent to a special friend
Who shares my laughter and regret
Whose friendship I shall never forget,
She lives in my worries, my hope and despair
For she or he will always be there.

Jessica McGill (11)
Hopelands School, Stonehouse

Cheetah

The fastest animal on the land
As the paw prints show among the sand,
The golden coat flashing in the sun,
As she hunts in the gleaming night for her daughter and son,
She jumps into the water to cool off her 22 spots,
When she sees some fishes like swirling dots,
Near the flowing river it their dark cosy den,
The cute, cuddly den but watching for men,
Whilst mum watches them from the treetops purring at them.

Jamie Douglas & Amiee Stone (10)
Huish Episcopi Primary School, Langport

Tiger

The prowler of the rainforest
While camouflaged against the grass
The wild animal stalks its prey
A beautiful meat eater
With roars as loud as an elephant stomping on the ground
With his big beady eyes he sneaks around the rainforests
The terrible tiger tears his food.
This ferocious beast is silent but deadly.

Holly Fraser & Lucy Cox (9)
Huish Episcopi Primary School, Langport

Tiger

This terrific tiger is as wise as a wizard
The stripy colours of the fur glows in the sun
Its fur so smooth and warm
Moments with the tiger is a treasure in your life
It prowls around trying to survive
The tiger soft paws pad silently on the ground
Friendly giving you a smile

Lily Coker (10)
Huish Episcopi Primary School, Langport

The Flame

The
Flame
Burning in
The air like
A raindrop splashing
On the ground
A forest of fire with burning
Leaves.
A snake's tongue hissing in the
Air. The flame like a rocket
Going up in the sky.
A boy splashing in a puddle
Of wax, and then
It dies.

Kieron Brain (9)
Huish Episcopi Primary School, Langport

The Flame

The
Flame
Like a burning
Raindrop, an orange
Leaf wiggling in the air,
A touch of light in the night
Sky, a tree melting in wax,
The snakes hissing louder
And louder, a rocket shooting up
And then
It dies.

Abbie Martin (9)
Huish Episcopi Primary School, Langport

I Like Summer

Summer is fun
Summer is young
I like summer it's fun.

Bees come out at summer
Birds come out to sing
That's why I like summer.

Swimming in the swimming pool
Seeing the sun pass by
Summer is fun, that's why.

Having a really nice barbecue
Sunbathing on the grass
Let's hope next summer
Is just as fun as this.

Katie Forrester (9)
Huish Episcopi Primary School, Langport

Our School Poem

Huish Episcopi Primary school
The teachers there are really cool
The Head is called Mrs Barraclough
By the end of the day she's out of puff
Mr Martin had to leave
Lots of presents he received
Mrs Mordue says bonjour when she walks through the door,
Mr Harnett teaches PE
He makes a great referee
Mr Shakesby loves to paint and draw
Egyptian faces on his wall
Miss Knifton is kind, gentle and really nice
She even smiles at the children's head lice.

Yasmin Webb (9)
Huish Episcopi Primary School, Langport

Goodnight, Sleep Tight Don't Let The Vampires Bite

When you go to sleep tonight
And your mother says goodnight
If you look out your window
It may give you a sudden fright
There's a shape, a shadow
Slowly slithers around the room
You pull the corner over your head
You look again, the window's shut
You give a sudden sigh of relief
But then a shape zooms out from
Under your bed, you faint
Your mother wakes you up in the morning
And she says, 'This place is a wreck,'
Then she notices in surprise
'What are those little holes in your neck?'

Edward Coate (9)
Huish Episcopi Primary School, Langport

Sweets

I went down the street one day
And all I have to say
Yum-yum I love sweets
I love the chocolate bars I eat
Sweets galore
All put in a tiny store.

I only have 90p
I wanted some sweets for me
I got a Twix
And some pic 'n' mix
I ate some Haribo
And I saw a rainbow.

Linden Derham (9)
Huish Episcopi Primary School, Langport

Fire

Hearing the crackle of the bonfire
Hearing the barbecue sizzle
Seeing the sparks fly up and down
Seeing the flames rise and rise
Feeling the heat on my face
Feeling the delicious hot dog between my teeth.
Smelling the burgers and bread
Smelling the smell of ashes
Guess who?
Fire!

Louis Jenkinson (9)
Huish Episcopi Primary School, Langport

Football

F unky trainers
O ver the goal
O n the head
T he one for me
B rilliant skills
A good goalkeeper
L ovely goals
L ow shots.

Michael Cox (9)
Huish Episcopi Primary School, Langport

Spring

S stands for sunny
P stands for puppies
R stands for rain
I stands for insets
N stands for nature
G stands for great.

Jade Beer (8)
Huish Episcopi Primary School, Langport

Nature

Rivers flowing slowly left
The sunny days are gone,
Baby animals are born today,
So let's all sing a song.
Wind swaying this and that
Windy days have come
Plants and trees are everywhere
So stay inside with mum!

Alice Bown (9)
Huish Episcopi Primary School, Langport

Spring's Nature

The sky so blue, makes the cows go 'moo',
The robins are singing, and the blue bells ringing,
As flowers grow, spring colours will show,
The grass is swaying, the lambs are playing,
The river is flowing and the flowers are growing,
The sun's so bright it gives a lovely light,
The birds are soaring, the rain's stopped pouring.
And spring is here!

Hannah Harris (9)
Huish Episcopi Primary School, Langport

My Cat

My cat is cute, my cat is kind
She's always loving as you will find
How will you know if you don't meet
That tabby cat on the street?
She walks with style, she walks with pride
With a smile on her face always giving a shine
But I definitely know she's mine, mine, mine.

Jasmine Stott (9)
Huish Episcopi Primary School, Langport

Sweets

Sweets, sweets,
Chocolate galore.

One of the things I adore
Twirls, Twixs and many more
All put together in a candy store.

When I open the door
Into the store
I lick my lips
At the pic 'n' mix

Sweets, sweets
Chocolate galore.

Charlie Keywood (8)
Huish Episcopi Primary School, Langport

River Parrot

River Parrot in all different parts
Seeing a chicken doing martial arts.
Kingfisher silvery blue
And all the roosters going cock-a-doodle-doo
Cheep, cheep a little chick.
I just ate fungus I'm going to be sick
A nest of swans white and sleek
. . . won't shut her beak.
A stop for lunch, a nice snack
That everybody forgot to pack
The end of the day is finally here
I forgot my bag, oh dear!

Gregory Watson (9)
Huish Episcopi Primary School, Langport

Circus

I went to the circus
I was really happy
I even met a seal called Slappy

I'm going to the circus, I'm going today
I'm going to the circus hip hip hooray!

When the clowns were on they
Were very funny!
The magician came on and had a bunny!

I'm going to the circus I'm going today
I'm going to the circus hip hip hooray!

It's the end of the circus it's the end of today
It's the end of the circus it's the end of the day!

Sinead Shephard (9)
Huish Episcopi Primary School, Langport

Nature

I saw the grass rustle
I saw the grass sway
I saw the grass cut
As I walked on my way

I saw the tree's branch
I saw the tree's roots
I saw the tree's bloom
As a flower droops

I saw the flower's stigma
I saw the flower's anther
I saw the flower's stem
As the zoo caught a panther.

Steven Langford (9)
Huish Episcopi Primary School, Langport

Ryan Giggs

R ed Devil's hero
Y our hero
A ttacker
N on stop scorer

G reat left foot
I ncredible skills
G reatness is unbelievable
G oodness is useful
S uper passing!

Matthew Joyner (9)
Huish Episcopi Primary School, Langport

Spring

S pring bring's the sun
P retty flower opening
R osy-red cheeks
I t's so hot
N ow it's getting dark
G o to bed!

Kayleigh Scadden (9)
Huish Episcopi Primary School, Langport

My Cousin Hilary

H er door is always open for troubles and concerns
I 'm spirited by her happiness her hair twists when she turns
L ying is impossible, because she's so honest
A nd never, ever boasts because she's always modest
R eady for whatever, is coming round the corner
Y ou're always safe with her so don't back away
                      you will be OK for every single day!

Abbie Bown (10)
Huish Episcopi Primary School, Langport

Teachers

Who knows how bees buzz?
Who knows French?
Who knows all the answers?
Mrs Mordue does.

Who knows how to draw rabbits?
Who knows loads of artists?
Who knows all the answers?
Mr Shakesby does.

Who knows how fast the world goes round?
Who knows how full the river is?
Who knows all the answers?
Mr Harnett does.

Belinda Massmann-Oakley (10)
Huish Episcopi Primary School, Langport

Music! Music! Music!

I adore music
I think it's really great
My favourite band
Busted of course!

I'm also amazed by Britney
I think she's rather pretty
She sings and dances
She does that a lot!

I absolutely love Avril
I think she's super cool
She jumps about with that guitar
Then she jumps to the floor.

Cara Sedgwick (9)
Huish Episcopi Primary School, Langport

Sweets

On a bright Sunday morning we pop down to the sweet shop and stare at the . . .
Cooking crazy Coke bottles
Curling Curly Wurly
White chocolate candy mice,
Don't leave one behind!
Twixs and Twixs, pic 'n' mixes
More and more
Chocolate and caramel galore.

I take a huge bag and eat and eat and eat!
One hour later
More and more 'Oh no,' I said
'I can't get out the door!'

Sophie Palmer (9)
Huish Episcopi Primary School, Langport

My New Pet

I have a new pet
I keep it in a hutch
It doesn't like getting wet
I like him very much.

My big cuddly bunny
It is a friendly boy
It's cute and funny
It's like a soft toy.

I clean it every day
He is my favourite creature
And I give it some fresh hay
He's almost like my teacher.

Hannah Lloyd (9)
Iron Acton CE Primary School, Bristol

My Brilliant Holiday

I'm going on holiday; I know there's a swimming pool
Just like every other holiday.
I'm going on holiday; we are going in a caravan
Just like every other holiday
I'm going on a boat; I know I'm going to be seasick
Just like every other holiday
I'm on the boat now; the boat's a ferry.
Just like every other holiday
I'm at the campsite now; we don't know the code to get in
Just like every other holiday
We have to find the owner, eventually we figured out the code.
Just like every other holiday
We set up the caravan now; it took us an hour.
Just like every other holiday.
I'm in the caravan now; I'm on the bottom bunk,
Just like every other holiday.
We are going to the swimming pool; I know there's water
Just like every other holiday
We're at the swimming pool now; I want to go down the water slide
Just like every other holiday
The water slide is really slow, it's quite boring
Just like every other holiday
We are going to the woods soon, it is going to be muddy
Just like every other holiday
We are in the woods now, I am really muddy
Just like every other holiday
There is a *trampoline!* I never knew that
Just like every other holiday
We have to go home, I do not want to
Just like every other holiday.

Alex Ashford (9)
Iron Acton CE Primary School, Bristol

My Holiday

Today I'm going on holiday
I think we're going camping
We've got to sleep in a damp old tent
It's going to be boring.

We're at the campsite now
There's nothing but other tents
I've got nothing to do
It's going to be boring.

It's already started to rain
And our campfire's gone out
My sister's started crying
It's going to be boring

It's *still* raining
Mum says it will be fun
Yeah right Mum
It's going to be boring

The sun's come out now
I've made a new friend
And Dad's in a good mood
I don't want this to end.

Ioni Bellis (9)
Iron Acton CE Primary School, Bristol

My Hamster

I've got a furry hamster
He's like a ball of fluff
Every time I touch him,
He goes to bite you if you're not careful
He likes being fed
He sleeps in a fluffy bed,
He wraps up tight
So then he can't bite
That's my Hammy Hamster!

Emma Pilgrim (10)
Iron Acton CE Primary School, Bristol

The Night Time Swimmer

One silent night when
There was not a sound
To be heard
It was silent.

I was in my boat as still as could be
I stopped breathing as I saw the swan
Drifting
Through the lake
Which was as calm as a blue sheet

Its feathers sparkled in the moonlight
Its beak was solid gold
And as orange as the sun
As it glided across the lake

It was a white glint floating away into the distance
But something was coming, as it came closer
I saw it was a swan feather.

For 6 years I have kept it as a good luck charm
I think
It was a gift given to me by the swan.

Richard Wiggins (10)
Iron Acton CE Primary School, Bristol

In The Great Green Garden

In the great green garden
There was a hideous hazel hutch
And in the hideous hazel hutch
There was a big black bunny
And in the big black bunny
There was fatty famous food
And in the fatty famous food
There was the slimy spicy sauce
And in the slimy spicy sauce
There was nothing, just nothing!

Rosie Brindle (10)
Iron Acton CE Primary School, Bristol

The Body

The body is a dusty, rusty, musty old piece of iron ore
People need to polish it more and more,
It helps us to live and stand up straight,
Our heart even has a pacey rate,
Our bones are very strong
To help us last long,
Our skull protects our brain,
So a crane doesn't smash it
The backbone protects the spinal nerve
So we don't get hurt when we swerve,
The tendon connects the muscle to the bone,
So we can bend our arm to hold the phone.

Seeing as we were given this excellent body,
Please don't lend it to anybody
If it breaks you won't get another one
So make good use of it whilst you have one.

Rebecca Barlow (10)
Iron Acton CE Primary School, Bristol

The Margalloof

The Margalloof is short and fat,
He'll dine upon a fine top hat,
A tie he'll eat with great pleasure
To him its like buried treasure
To have the privilege of eating a suit,
He'll eat the shoe right off your foot.

The Margalloof leaves his initial,
Marked in slime and bits of spittle,
If you find an 'M' upon your head
You must rise from your comfy bed,
Find your wardrobe, check your clothes
The margalloof is a creature to loathe.

Alistair Mansfield (10)
Iron Acton CE Primary School, Bristol

School Day

The school day starts at five to nine
All the classes stand in line.
We go in to get our books out.
Hear the teacher start to shout!

We start our literacy all sat down
We started a poem about a town
There was a boy with eighteen toes
And one huge knobbly nose.

'Come on class its time for break
Please children, not in the lake'
We run around playing 'tag'.
Then my mum comes up with a PE bag.

Then we all rush in from 'Tag'
Trying hard to find our bag
Then we get out our spelling book
I see the teacher start to look.

We all stand eager to go home
We want to watch a programme on Rome
Mum's stood waiting that's the end
As we turn around the bend.

Hannah Byrne (9)
Iron Acton CE Primary School, Bristol

Bunnies

Bunnies are fluffy, loving and sweet,
They jump up and down and act like clowns,
With fur so soft that you want to touch,
Twitching noses, silly long ears, I love them so much.
Their white cottontails puff out like clouds,
I want them all tucked up in my bed
As you all know I am not allowed
Oh little bunnies come live with me,
You will have plenty of food and cuddles
Have trust in me.

Devon Kimberley (9)
Iron Acton CE Primary School, Bristol

My Cat Pat

I've got a cat
She is called Pat
She is very bad
She winds up my dad
Pat goes out
She hasn't got a snout
She plays with another cat
Her name is Nat
She likes playing with her
Because she has a lot of fur.

Sadie Perks (8)
Iron Acton CE Primary School, Bristol

Animals

A snake
There was a snake
That smelt of cake
And he was called Bake
He was soft and squiddgy like a sponge
He smelt good enough to eat
He's better than a parakeet
And the parakeet didn't smell sweet.

The p*arrot*
There was a parrot
Who ate loads of magical carrots
And he always laughed
He never had a bath
He was smarter then a brain
He always loved playing with a toy crane
He hated it when it rained
He always bumped his head
And he could never get out of bed.

Chris Appleton (10)
Longborough CE Primary School, Moreton-In-Marsh

The Clown

Big red nose, brightly coloured clothes
Humongous shoes, what tricks will he choose
So many balls go juggling round
Round and round again . . .

A middle-sized hat just to fit him
When his show starts they turn the lights dim
Everyone loves him, they scream and shout
When some people are jealous they just look and pout
He is the funniest man in the world
He makes me want to laugh out loud
And shout to everyone
'Come and see the clown!'

Emma Cook (8)
Longborough CE Primary School, Moreton-In-Marsh

Seasons

Friends are what bring that wintry cheer
Which keeps you warm this time of year
Let's go skating, it's winter!

Spring is on its way
Sunshine smiles, new baby flowers and buzzing bees

Summer season of adventure
Flowers smell sweet as honey
There's no such thing as too much money!

It's autumn and it's raining leaves!
Weather turns cold - leaves turn gold
The woods are awash with autumn.

Rachel Deane (9)
Longborough CE Primary School, Moreton-In-Marsh

Teachers

Most teachers are boring
Some teachers are cool
Some teachers are smelly!
Some teachers I don't like at all!

Some teachers are naughty
Some teachers are good
My teacher was shouting
But I understood!

Some teachers are bossy
Some teachers are kind
There are hardly any gracious ones
As they're very hard to find!

Art is my favourite lesson
I like painting best
I don't like drawing at all
It really is a pest!

Miss Rosy and Mrs O teach us
They make the lessons fun
Sometimes we do art outside
And we enjoy ourselves in the sun!

I enjoy art because
Miss Rosy and Mrs O aren't boring
They make the lessons exciting
And they keep us all from snoring!

Lily Willcocks (10)
Longborough CE Primary School, Moreton-In-Marsh

Chance

There was a man called Lance
He really took a chance
He bought a bun
Stuck it up his gun
And fired it over sea to France.

Alex Dewhurst (10)
Longborough CE Primary School, Moreton-In-Marsh

The Hell's Angels

They're fast, they're cool, they're big and strong
They're the Hell's Angels
They have big bikes that were built for speed
They're the Hell's Angels
They ride here, they ride there, they ride everywhere,
They're the Hell's Angels
They eat everything, they sleep in their clothes
They're the Hell's Angels
They eat slugs, they eat snails, they eat worms as big as you and me
They're the Hell's Angels
They sleep on the side of the road, they sleep in the bins
They're the Hell's Angels
They drink all day, they drink all night
They're the Hell's Angels
They're rough, tough and bad enough
They're the Hell's Angels
They ride Harleys, Triumphs and BSAs
They're the Hell's Angels
They have no house, they have no inn
They're the Hell's Angels.

Nathan Long (10)
Longborough CE Primary School, Moreton-In-Marsh

Nature

Rustling leaves in the forests
Rabbits running wild
The fresh green grass on the fields
Foxes hiding from ruthless hunters
Pheasants eating the seeds
Birds whistling an enchanting melody
The hikers marching over the meadow
Animals galloping like stallions
Zooming jets and the golden sun over the hills.

Samuel Mazur (11)
Longborough CE Primary School, Moreton-In-Marsh

The Silly French Man

There was an old man from France
Who had a love for plants
He ran around France
Squashed all his plants
While doing a country dance

He grew them back
Fell on a sack
Squashed them again and said
'I am going to bed.'

Ted Turvey (11)
Longborough CE Primary School, Moreton-In-Marsh

The Rich Witch

There once was a headless witch
Who had a pet ostrich
She sold it to a man
Who had a big red van
And then she was terribly rich.

Amber Griffin (11)
Longborough CE Primary School, Moreton-In-Marsh

Dead Red Turtle

There once was a woman called Myrtle
Who once has a pet pink turtle
She painted it red
And then it was dead
So watch out for a dead red turtle.

Jade Temple (10)
Longborough CE Primary School, Moreton-In-Marsh

There Once Was A Boy Called Rick

There once was a boy called Rick
He slipped on a very big brick
He broke his back
Got put in a sack
And he died from a heart attack

He went to heaven
Which was close to Devon
He saw his cat,
Which was eating a rat
And the cat was extremely fat.

Rick saw his friend Ben,
Who was laying a hen,
He thought this was weird
Because he had grown a beard
So he gave up and said
'I'm going to bed.'

Kyle Ellery (11)
Longborough CE Primary School, Moreton-In-Marsh

The War Poem

I was lying on that beach
I was sighing on that beach
I was crying on that beach
I felt I was dying on that beach

I could smell smoke, blood and bones
I was lying in the mud and stones.
When suddenly someone spoke
'Soon you will be dead,' he said
'Goodbye,' I said
Now I am dead.

George Stuckey (10)
Lovington CE VC Primary School, Somerset

D-Day

I thought wars were only fought by other people
Meant for someone else but not for me
Now the Germans have shot me,
And most of my friends are down too.

I wish I never joined the armed forces.

It's like a dream,
No - more like a nightmare
My squadron must have thought I was dead.
They've left me here alone with only dead bodies for company
Well I do feel dead, smell dead and look dead,
So it's an easy mistake to make,
But still, you should never abandon your mates.

The tide is coming in.
It's about the only thing I can feel -
I can hear it washing away the bodies
I can't get up so I'll be the next one to die
Carelessly washed away by the tide
I'm drifting in and out of consciousness.

I hope I've done something to help in the war

I hope it will end soon.

Emma Simmonds (11)
Lovington CE VC Primary School, Somerset

World War

W hy must we go to war? For it
O nly brings carnage and
R epugnance. I can still see the
L oathing in our opponents as they
D estroyed us one by one.

W hen I awoke, my friends were nowhere to be seen,
A s my air slowly
R an out, I greeted Death's scythe warmly.

Ben Talbot (10)
Lovington CE VC Primary School, Somerset

The Morning After D-Day

It is daybreak the day after D-Day
It is sunny and I can feel the warmth on my face
And hear the sounds of the sea
The waves are much calmer then yesterday
I feel sad -
All my squadron have moved on and left me alone.

I can still hear the machine guns and rifles,
Loud and very close.

Leaning up against a roll of barbed wire,
I can feel the barbs pressing against my chest and legs.
I've been shot . . .
I can't move my leg.
My uniform is soaked with blood and pain.

I can see soldiers looking frightened and
Falling to the ground in pain.

Oliver Veryard (10)
Lovington CE VC Primary School, Somerset

D-Day

I woke up and saw a terrible sight
No more battle on the field
My men had departed, they thought I was dead
I tried to walk but I just toppled over.

I heard a terrible noise
Then a Sherman tank came up behind me
And boom! Rat-tat-tat, argh!
I saw the grim darkness of eternal rest grab me

Then I was gone forever . .

Tom Tubridy (10)
Lovington CE VC Primary School, Somerset

Waiting

I'm lying here on the beach -
Where they left me
I think I need some help
I keep thinking of my girl back home.

I'm not gonna make it.
The air is filled with the smell of death
I've just got to focus on one thing -
The Germans are coming!
They're coming in their tanks.

I'm a goner.
How much more can I take?
Argh! . . . Now I can see the sea,
Covered in what looks like a thick black oil,
No - it's actually ships.

Screams fill my ears, screams from my friends
Tick . . . tick . . . tick . . . a bomb
I've got to get up and run . . . can't move my leg
I need to shout for help but I can't speak . . .

The pain has gone.
I am gone.
Slipping away, out of reach.

Jade Glover (11)
Lovington CE VC Primary School, Somerset

I'm A Soldier

I'm a soldier
I didn't want to be one, but I had no choice.
I am a wounded soldier, on a lonely and dead beach.
With other badly wounded allied soldiers.
My rifle is battle-damaged with scratch marks from the shots
That missed me.

Blood from the soldiers is spreading all around
And drifting into the rough sea
I feel half dead, dragging my rifle around
The darkish red half-dead beach
The tanks are coming, ramming me from behind.
They finally kill me

I wasn't the only one.

Kane Clarke (11)
Lovington CE VC Primary School, Somerset

The Army Man

The army man could hear screeching from the seagulls
He heard children running and screaming,
                                      trying to get away if they could.
He was covered in blood from head to toe,
He had ripped clothes and the sand was cold and wet,
He could smell the salty smell of the waves crashing
                                against the rocks and the seaweed.
The man was dying
He was scared and thinking about his family
Then he was gone.

Amanda Matthews (10)
Lovington CE VC Primary School, Somerset

The Sound Of The Sea

Lying on the crowded, noisy beach
The air is filled with fire and smoke, and the crackle of machine guns.
The only thing calming me is the gentle sound of the sea.

Tanks click around me. Every now and then one explodes
Molten metal melts like silver-green ice out of the bottom;
With the sound of the sea coming closer.

There is a dead soldier lying next to me.
Or is he? I don't know
Dead or alive he looks in pain.
The sound of the sea comes closer.

In the morning I wake up.
I am in a different place . . .
And the sea is all around me.

Jake Witherington (11)
Lovington CE VC Primary School, Somerset

World War Two

I can see an aeroplane having a battle with another one
                             and then it's falling from the sky.
I can see a house being bombed and everyone screaming,
                             and running away.
I can hear big bangs from the bombs and
                             the sea crashing against the rocks.
I can hear people screaming and shouting trying to get away
I can smell the smoke from guns and bombs
I can smell my dirty uniform and the sea salt
I am going, fading away. I fall onto my knees,
                             I am cold and wet, and in pain.
I am thinking about my family.

Libby Graham (10)
Lovington CE VC Primary School, Somerset

Death Is Near

I wake up feeling weak
My friend is lying dead
I hear screams
And I feel very sad
The seagulls are pecking at me with their beaks.

Awake now, I feel cold
Not at all brave
Most are dead
Some in hospital
I smell lots of smoke

I long for a ship
The letter my mum wrote
My love is at home
I want to be with her
I feel cold and would like a blanket.

Harriet Ffooks (10)
Lovington CE VC Primary School, Somerset

D-Day

The men in the boat waited
The shore was close
They waited patiently
A plane passed overhead
Boom!
They tumbled into red water
Machine guns
Men screaming for cover
Struggling to swim for shore
The feel of coldness.

Tommy Reynolds (9)
Lovington CE VC Primary School, Somerset

Abandoned

I could smell the rotten mouldy scent of bones and soil
The tanks were burning and the smell of death was in the air,
No one in the world knew, no one to care.

The sounds of gunfire echoed through my mind
I was still there where my squad had left me.
Alone in the world lying next to the sea.

The waves were roaring like the Germans' weapons
The bare wasteland surrounded me like the German troops,
One last gunfire, one last shot.

Stephanie Thayer (10)
Lovington CE VC Primary School, Somerset

Guess Who?

Controller-snatcher
Mean-scratcher
Lazy-sleeper
Sneaky-sneaker
Baby-sitter
Greedy-gobbler
Mess-maker
Mud-trailer
Rough-fighter
Pond-fiddler
Game-wrecker
Annoying-meddler
Class-fidgeter
Scruffy-writer
TV-hogger
Sweetie-stealer

Answer: Brothers

Eleanor Kelly (10)
Mitton Manor Primary School, Tewkesbury

Guess Who?

Tail wagger
Sense sniffer
Great player
Bone digger
Greedy eater
Thirsty slurper
Stroll walker
Rapid runner
Noise maker
High jumper
Big licker
Aggressive growler
Snoozy sleeper
Tired panter
Cat chaser
Lead puller.

Answer: Golden Retriever

Annie Wilkinson (10)
Mitton Manor Primary School, Tewkesbury

Guess What?

Long-leaper
Excellent-swimmer
Egg-layer
Human-frightener
Lilly pad-sitter
Female-finder
Fly-eater
Noisy-croaker
Sneaky-hider

Answer: Frog

Wayne Greening (9)
Mitton Manor Primary School, Tewkesbury

Guess Who?

Paper ball chaser
Curtain climber
Photo modeller
Tail swinger
Fur moulter
Silent stalker
Patient predator
Coat licker
Fish taunter
Tightrope walker
Fussy groomer
Attention seeker
Lap sitter
Cuddle lover

Answer: Kittens

Chloe Mason (10)
Mitton Manor Primary School, Tewkesbury

Guess Who?

Tear crier
Noisy liar
Mean kicker
Nasty fighter
Good arguer
Loud screamer
Make-up stealer
Bad criticiser
Tantrum thrower

Answer: Sisters

Elena Amadeo (9)
Mitton Manor Primary School, Tewkesbury

Guess What I Am?

Mad jumper
Horrible eater
Noisy drinker
Fast runner
Nasty biter
Rough scratcher
Bad fighter
Slow walker
Loud growler
Tasty chomper
Smooth barker
Weird panter
Soft licker
Naughty chewer
Funny smiler

Answer: Dog

Jessica Perry (9)
Mitton Manor Primary School, Tewkesbury

What Am I?

Lifesaver
Blood taker
Insulin Injector
Bed maker
Temperature taker
People helper
Care giver
Bandage wrapper
Wheelchair pusher
Risk taker
Pulse checker

Answer: Nurse

Elly King (9)
Mitton Manor Primary School, Tewkesbury

Guess What?

Safari wrecker
Wild chatterer
Banana eater
Jungle swinger
Loose hanger
High jumper
Quick leaper
Good hider
Great stealer
Cool lunger
Arm pit itcher
Team player
Big cheetah

Answer: Monkey

Roseanna Davis (10)
Mitton Manor Primary School, Tewkesbury

Guess What?

Springs jumper
Hungry eater
Water drinker
Dribble licker
Heavy sleeper
Noisy barker
Tail wager
Ear scratcher
Cry whimper

Answer: Dog

Kiera Newborough (10)
Mitton Manor Primary School, Tewkesbury

Guess What?

Loud panter
Tail wagger,
Naughty growler
Fast runner,
Good sniffer
Messy muncher,
High jumper
Noisy barker,
Lead puller
Ball fetcher,
Bone digger
Cat chaser!

Answer: Dog

Jessica Bouwer (9)
Mitton Manor Primary School, Tewkesbury

Guess What?

Loud shouter
Fast runner
High jumper
Tree swinger
Big growler
Banana lover
Banana peeler
Bouncy dancer
Chest banger
Tree hanger.

Answer: Chimp

Lauren Grainger (10)
Mitton Manor Primary School, Tewkesbury

Guess What I Am

Top-jumper
Naughty-growler
Ear-flapper
Walk-lover
Big-licker
Food-gobbler
Drink-lapper
Bone-finder
Great-player
Ball-popper
Stick-fetcher
Rapid-runner
Treat-nicker
Hand-biter
Tail-wagger
Heavy-sleeper
Noise-maker
Attention-seeker

Answer: Cocker Spaniel

Lizzie Clarke (10)
Mitton Manor Primary School, Tewkesbury

Guess Who?

Loud sleeper
Throat growler
Sprint runner
High leaper
Hungry eater
Quiet hunter
Slow drinker

Answer: Tiger

Ben Carter (10)
Mitton Manor Primary School, Tewkesbury

Guess What?

Fierce roarer
Tasty chewer
Greedy eater
Jungle leader
Rough scratcher
Fast chaser
Speedy sprinter
Cheerful leaper
Mad pouncer
Long strider
Lazy lazer
Tired sleeper
Steady hunter
Cheeky sneaker
And you can't forget
Proud fighter

Answer: Lion

Tom Allcoat (10)
Mitton Manor Primary School, Tewkesbury

Guess What?

60 miles per hour sprinter
Cub breeder
Cheeky sneaker
Lazy snorer
Antelope hunter
Silent hunter
Midnight howler
Meal sharer
Zebra prowler
Playful fighter
Quick thinker

Answer: Cheetah

Sam Gaisford (10)
Mitton Manor Primary School, Tewkesbury

Guess Who?

TV watcher
Pig outer
Fast slapper
Food fisher
Speedy cooker
School hater
Maniac computer
Slow eater
Quick gobbler
World traveller
Long fighter
Iron timer
Washer upper
Shed fixer
House cleaner
Nappy changer
Bedroom tidier
Pop star lover
Bedroom remover
Car collector
Fuss maker
Candy buyer
Puppy wanter
Gardener maker
Fence painter

Answer: Family

Helen Thompson (9)
Mitton Manor Primary School, Tewkesbury

Guess What I Am?

Feet stomper
Trunk waver
Ear flapper
Human helper
Loud trumpeter
Woodland searcher
Excellent thinker
Quick drinker
Loud eater
Brilliant swimmer
Fast slurper
Music maker
Safari walker

Answer: Elephant

Samantha Danter (10)
Mitton Manor Primary School, Tewkesbury

Guess What I Am?

Soft neigher
Deep sleeper
Cheeky grinner
Messy roller
Strong fighter
High jumper
Sloppy drinker
Loud snorter
Food gobbler
Noise maker
Fast galloper

Answer: Horse

Katherine Nash (9)
Mitton Manor Primary School, Tewkesbury

Guess Who?

Loud shouter
Book reader
Hand holder
Child lover
Cheek kisser
Big hugger
Car driver
Long talker
Homework helper
Wine drinker
Food cooker
Baby sitter
Hair brusher
Story teller
Letter writer
Money spender
Face wiper
Problem solver
House cleaner
Make-up user

Answer: Mum

Ellen Kettell (9)
Mitton Manor Primary School, Tewkesbury

Who Am I?

Leg tackler
Top scorer
Professional passer
Great shooter
Dirty fouler
Skilful diver
Careful dribbler
Long thrower
Athletic runner
Goal saver
Money lover
Speedy sprinter
Hard player
Ball hogger
Beckham bender
Carlos curler
Exciting vollier
Powerful header
Rule breaker
Player dodger
Play actor.

Answer: Footballer

Sam Rayner (10)
Mitton Manor Primary School, Tewkesbury

Guess Who?

Thumb sucker
Car pusher
Room messer
Biscuit eater
Crumb maker
Sweet stealer
Teeth gaper
Showing off at supper
Smile cheeker
Playing tricks on mother

Answer: Brothers

Owen Vincent (9)
Mitton Manor Primary School, Tewkesbury

Guess What?

High jumper
Fast swimmer
Fly lover
Women frightener
Lazy sitter
Clumsy crosser
Noisy croaker
Hungry eater
Sunbather
Thirsty drinker
Egg layer

Answer: Frog

Baptiste Nottingham (10)
Mitton Manor Primary School, Tewkesbury

Guess What?

Tail wagger
Face licker
Tongue loller
Mouth dribbler
Food eater
Water drinker
Biscuit biter
Long walker
Fast runner
Hand biter
Leg scratcher
Carpet sleeper

Answer: Dog

Olivor Francis (9)
Mitton Manor Primary School, Tewkesbury

Guess Who?

High jumper
Carrot muncher
Naughty nipper
Fast runner
Grass eater
Nose twitcher
Sudden pouncer
Bottom dropper
Foot hopper
Huge listener
Dozy sleeper

Answer: Rabbit

Emma Williams (10)
Mitton Manor Primary School, Tewkesbury

Guess What!

Bone muncher
Fire flamer
Back spiker
Swift flyer
Enemy melter
Smoke breather
Food nipper
Giant killer
Sky sailer
Tired panter
Slime scaler

Answer: Dragon

Tom Lewis (10)
Mitton Manor Primary School, Tewkesbury

Guess What!

Deadly killer
Breath suffocater
Slimy slither
Bone crusher
Creature squeezer
Springy coiler
Mean fighter
Animal eater
Slick swimmer
Mysterious hisser
Tongue poker
Slow mover
Trapping constrictor

Answer: Anaconda

Sam Gray (10)
Mitton Manor Primary School, Tewkesbury

Guess What I Am

Ear-flapper
Feet-stomper
Bottom-trumper
Body-swayer
Food-sucker
Mud-roller
Nose-swinger
Tail-flinger
Skin-bather
People-watcher
Water-shooter
Charging-fighter

Answer: Elephant

Laura Griffin (10)
Mitton Manor Primary School, Tewkesbury

My Dream

If I could dream an exciting dream
Filled with excitement and dare
My fantasies
Would not be questioned
I wouldn't have a single worry or care.
My imagination
Would drive me wherever
I want to go,
Giving fulfilment to my life
That was spare
My spirit would roam free floating anywhere
And not bother about anything.
I would daydream
Forever of having long, white wings.
If this was reality, which it is not
Would I have wings? I think not

Tasmin Jones (10)
Pauntley CE Primary School, Newent

The Christmas Bird

The Christmas bird
With an orange chest
Stands out from all the rest.

Its little beak
Full of song
Can hold a note for so long.

It hops around
From branch to branch,
Not missing its little chance
To catch a worm
From the ground
And not let it move around.

She shares it out
For the young
And how grateful they are
For what she's brung.

Chewed then swallowed
That's how it's done
Until it has all gone

The baby robin
May not live long
But it's got a beautiful chest
And a lovely song.

Danielle Trevail (11)
Pauntley CE Primary School, Newent

My Grandad

My grandad is the master of time
He sings a lot of songs and he repeats a lot of rhymes.

My grandad is a warm, calm man and he loves to talk
But my, my there was never a grandad
Who was one to walk as much as my grandad

He's walked in Canada, in España, he's even walked in Malaga
On the planes where he lives in Spain

My grandad is the best artist ever,
He's tops and he's ever so clever,
He comes from England but he lives in Spain
And now he's ill, it's a great shame.

I wouldn't swap my grandad for any other,
Because he's the father of my mother
And my grandad is master of time
He sings a lot of songs and he repeats a lot of rhymes.

Luke Hodgin (11)
Pauntley CE Primary School, Newent

The Moon

The moon rises and swallows the light
The moon rises and spits out the stars
The moon rises and goes fast
Like Ronaldo kicking the moon around the world
It's like a banana bed in the air
The moon sneaks and eats the sun
In the morning the moon coughs
The moon sinks down to the bottom of the earth in the morning.

Josh Hunt
Pendock CE Primary School, Pendock

The Moon

The moon rises
To push the sun out of the sky
It gets smaller and smaller
To see everybody sleeping.

The moon glows and sparkles
The sun jumps from the moon
It makes it run away
It's a ball of snow.

The moon quietly and secretly
Comes up in the sky
It's completely round and looks like a circle
It collapses in the morning

The moon drops down
Then the sun jumps up
The moon jumps to the night
In a different world.

Emma Mealing (9)
Pendock CE Primary School, Pendock

The Moon

The moon rises up on the world
To see the people awake.

The moon glows and shimmers
Like the biggest disco ball.

The moon glows like
A Hallowe'en pumpkin.

The moon is heavy as ninety elephants.

Jade Taylor
Pendock CE Primary School, Pendock

The Moon

The moon rises
It creeps and lights up the sky
Telling the people it's night
It's like a shining lump of silver

The moon
Sparkles like a glitter ball
Spins round and round to spit out light

The moon sneaks up on the sun
It chases the sun along the gloomy sky
It runs around like a rat

The moon sinks down to Earth
It hits the ground like a bouncy ball
A lump of ioo in the sky.

Katie Leigh
Pendock CE Primary School, Pendock

The Moon

The moon rises
And swallows the stars

The moon sparkles
Like a disco ball
It's like a fat rubber

The moon spooks the sun
And hits the baking hot sun
The moon pushes the sun away.

The moon is like a great big
Ball of cheese
And turns like a fish.

Isobel Williams (8)
Pendock CE Primary School, Pendock

The Moon

The moon rises
Swallows the light and the sun
Like a big mouth
Night-time and bedtime, zzzzzz

The moon rises
Like a knight in glittering armour
In the night sky.

The moon creeps
Pops up like a jack-in-the-box
Out of the sky.

The moon slips
Like someone falling from the sky
Daytime.

Rhiannon King (7)
Pendock CE Primary School, Pendock

The Moon

The moon jumps up in the night surprising the sleeping sun
It watches the people
Like a digital camera filming people.

The moon glows in the darkness
Like a Hallowe'en prank
A ghost
A white bouncy ball

The moon is pale white
Like a shocked man
Dennis the Menace when he sees the flowers
A mouse when he sees a cat.

Ryan Keyte (9)
Pendock CE Primary School, Pendock

The Moon

The moon rises
And glitters over the world below
And chases the stars around
And shines like a silver ball in the sky.

The moon
Is like a silver 3D pizza
But it has no pepperoni
And it makes the wolves howl.

The moon
Travels along the galaxy
Swallowing the stars
Like little sweets

Thomas Jones
Pendock CE Primary School, Pendock

The Moon's Time Line

The moon rises
And burps out the stars.

The moon glitters
Like a lump of body glitter in the sky.

The moon sneaks
Like people out at you.

The moon collapses
In the sudden sunrise.

Chloe Darrell
Pendock CE Primary School, Pendock

The Moon

The moon is like a white banana frozen
And a shiny sword shining in the sky
It's like a glitter ball
And it's the queen in the sky.

The moons like a disco light cut in half
And it's like a big white shell
It's like a gloomy pony.

The moons like a sea of light
As heavy as a million elephants in a pile
As hot as a pan in a toaster.

It's like a shimmer glow
It's like a person.

Holly Neal (8)
Pendock CE Primary School, Pendock

The Moon

The moon rises and swallows the light
Which surprises the sun
The stars sparkle in the sky next to the moon.

The moon sparkles like a huge mirror ball in the night sky.
The moon sneaks through the night sky
Like a robber in the middle of a robbery.

The moon sinks down from the morning sun
The sun pops up and surprises the moon
Like the moon had done earlier.

Kiya Hughes
Pendock CE Primary School, Pendock

The Moon

The moon rises and sparkles
It shimmers like a big disco ball and its like a diamond

The moon glitters like a beautiful big diamond
Like a gorgeous big, lovely, sparkly ball
Like a beautiful shimmering nice hair curl

The moon shimmers like a glittering ball and like a hair curl
Like a disco ball like a diamond.

The moon is like a shimmering sword
Like a hair curl
And like a diamond
Like a disco ball.

The moon is like a shimmering sword
Like an eye
Like a glittering sword
Like a dog's eye.

Jordan-Marie Welsh
Pendock CE Primary School, Pendock

The Moon

The moon rises
Up in the sky
Glittering down upon the world

The moon sparkles
Down by the sea
The dolphins jumping about
Out of the water.

The moon creeps
And pushes the sun away
Then hides behind the hills.

Sophie Eggerton
Pendock CE Primary School, Pendock

The Moon

The moon bounces up into the sky
And spits out the glittery stars.

The players play hide-and-seek with the sun
And every time the moon wins.

The moon glitters
Shows off because it always wins.

But this time the sun wins
And the moon goes crashing down to the ground
And then it is morning.

Cameron Dallimore
Pendock CE Primary School, Pendock

Fun Friendship

F is for friends playing together
U is for u and me
N is for never having rows.

F is for friendly help
R is for rough bullies being chased away
I is for individual
E is for everlasting fun
N is for never having to ask
D is for day or night
S is for special mates
H is for happy days
I is for impact on happiness
P is for playing together forever.

Katherine Voysey (11)
Perry Court Junior School, Hengrove

Storm

I turn and tear trashing every place
I earthquake everywhere there is a space
I earthquake people unit they cry
And quickly smack them until they die.

I howl like a wolf in the full moon
And smash lots of glass like an evil baboon
I whirlpool people so they know who's boss
And then I'll give them a mighty big toss.

I'm clouds of lightning filling the air
And then I get angry and decide to scare
I tidal wave people when they bug me
Using all the water from the sea.

Joshua Vowles (9)
Perry Court Junior School, Hengrove

Storm

I made a dark cloud to block the sun
I made tatty twisters turn into terror
Twirling, whirling tearing towns apart but then
I became tired and stopped.
I lifted my colossal arm and crashed down to Earth
I made a gigantic volcano erupt and it looked
                                       like a mad dragon spitting fire.
I made terrible thunder in the night and it sounded like thousands
                                       of asteroids crashing down to earth
I made vital floods cover the face of the Earth
I made an earthquake by pushing a giant down the stairs
Now the day has ended I plan for tomorrow.

Jordan Edwards (10)
Perry Court Junior School, Hengrove

Miserable

M oaning and groaning
I n your house
S itting on the sofa
E ating Brussels sprouts
R abbiting on at your mum
A bout a difficult sum
B eing a pain
L aughing and shouting
E very day and every way.

Jordan Davies (11)
Perry Court Junior School, Hengrove

Sudden Thunder

Suddenly a grey black cloud poured over England
Then bang clatter, rumble in England
I will be thunder, me thunder, well I will invade England
I went to Cornwall and scared dozens of people
I came back to Bristol and spoilt the nice weather
Everyone ran inside
Then it came to the end of the day.

Colby Avent (9)
Perry Court Junior School, Hengrove

Thunder

I'm the thrashing thunder making people scared by crashing
I bang like a big bass drum in the night
I slash the tiles with my friend lightening.
I'm like a crash in the middle of a stormy night
In the morning I will go to sleep and on a rough night
I will come out and scare people out of their skin
I live in the sky the big boring blazing sky
I'm the furious weather.

Max Pearce (10)
Perry Court Junior School, Hengrove

Best Friend

B oyfriends, girlfriends come and go
E ach time someone new
S pecial friends stay together
T ogether like me and you.

F riendship is forever
R unning, playing games
I mmensely fun you are to me
E ach of the jokes and funny names
N ow stick with me, I like you heaps
D ecision, you're my best friend for keeps.

Emily Butler (11)
Perry Court Junior School, Hengrove

The Sun

I flow through the sky like kites in the breeze,

I melt people's ice cream out of spite

Because I don't get the sweet taste of the flavour,

I glow as radiant as a torch at night,

I glisten down on the river shimmering on the sunset.

Sophie Higgins, Kayla Whippey & Natalie Wookey (10)
Perry Court Junior School, Hengrove

Flowers

F lowers are pretty
L ovely for all
O nly when it's summer
W ill they grow
E very day
R ain or sun
S miley faces all around.

Aaron Meredith (11)
Perry Court Junior School, Hengrove

School In May

Do I have to do SATs?
Do I have to go to school?
Do I have to be a good girl?
Do I have to go by the rules?

Do I have to have hot dinners?
Even though they're yummy,
Flapjack and cake, on my plate
Are better in my tummy.

And how about English?
And do I have to perform nice writing?
I don't like reading comprehension
The whole thing's quite frightening!

Maths is just as bad
With complicated angles.
Perimeter and area,
And different shaped triangles.

Science is the worse,
With liquids, solids and gases.
Germination and pollination
And which force works the fastest.

By the end of May,
All is said and done
SATs are finally over
And I'm having fun!

Lucy Hacker (11)
Perry Court Junior School, Hengrove

Dolphin Haiku

Dolphins are graceful
They glide through the deep blue sea
Diving through the air.

Emily Brown (11)
Perry Court Junior School, Hengrove

The Rain

I form grey clouds when I pitter-patter on the ground -
A puddle I have conjured

I started as a small April shower
But got heavier as my temper progressed

I tumble from the sky
Like a young child learning to walk.

I splash off windows and dribble down drains
I thud on windows, as people get drenched

People run for cover as they see me coming nearer
I overflow rivers and cause massive floods
The clouds that I conjure are as black as burning coal.

Kayleigh Clark, Paige Tripp-Edwards, Leah Fisher (10)
Perry Court Junior School, Hengrove

The Wind

I am a violent destroyer
An accassin of the people
I am fast and fearless
I rage round and round
I'm like an enraged bull
I'm a dinosaur on the loose
I will destroy anything in my path
I have the power of a bomb
I am faster than a plane
I am a fist of destruction
I am the almighty wind.

James Perry & Jacob Pocock (10)
Perry Court Junior School, Hengrove

My Pets

I have a pet called Gizzy
She is rather dizzy
I have a pet called Patch
He always loves to scratch
I have a pet called Mo
He is rather slow.

Gizzy is a dog
She sleeps like a log.
Patch is a guinea pig
His fur looks like a wig
Mo is his brother
Who is nothing like the other.

Gizzy loves a walk,
And sometimes tries to talk.
Patch is rather shy
And hopes you'll pass him by.
Mo will bite
But only in a fright

These are my pets
I take them to the vets
When they are ill
I give them a pill.

I love my pets so much
I like to hold and touch
They are very special to me
They are my friends, all three.

Carly Thomas (11)
Perry Court Junior School, Hengrove

My Little Friend Haiku

Fluttering feathers
Fly zigzagging through the sky
While she sings loudly.

Sophia Mulvihill (8)
St John's Catholic Primary School, Bath

Phoenix

Phoenix
Like a front page
To life or death
A brave warrior
A slayer of evil
Eyes of flame
Peace in the body of a bird.

Phoenix
A bird to be reckoned with
Repairer of broken hearts
Harm need not be with you
With the phoenix at your back
It's duty done now
A grave of ashes
But from those ashes
A new guardian arises.

Tom Morris (10)
St John's Catholic Primary School, Bath

A Tall Tree Haiku

He stands tall and straight
Everyone looks up to him
And they feel happy.

Steven Pearce (8)
St John's Catholic Primary School, Bath

Fairies Haiku

Glitter fairies fly
Above our heads in the sky
Giving luck to us.

Sophie Teasdale (8)
St John's Catholic Primary School, Bath

The Wobbly Jelly

Why does jelly, wobble on a plate?
Why are children always late?

Why is rain always wet?
Why are fish caught in nets?

Why are rocks always hard?
Are there such things as Easter cards?

Why do dogs, bark, bark, bark?
Why do teachers mark, mark, mark?

Why are books so hard to read?
Why do dogs need their leads?

Why are lines always straight?
Why do sharks eat cold bait?

Phoebe Langley (10)
St John's Catholic Primary School, Bath

I Am The Palms

People grab hold of me,
Clasp me tight,
From the break of dawn,
Till the start of night.

Meeting life,
Meeting death,
The one, the only
Holy man's breathe.

The Father, the Son
The Spirit of Holy,
Riding through the street,
Incredibly, slowly.

Anna Piercy (11)
St John's Catholic Primary School, Bath

Penguins

Penguins,
Living in the icy seas,
Diving deep,
Their white tummies
And black wings.

Penguins
Waddling across the snow,
Sitting by the water's edge.
Waiting to dive into the cold waters,
Of the Atlantic ocean.

Alice Piekarski (10)
St John's Catholic Primary School, Bath

My Spell

Human's brains, liver and all,
Body of fly squashed by ball
A tiger's roar and leopard's spot,
Old man's false teeth, teachers' snot.
Pelican's beak, toucan's wing,
Eyeball and nose from England's king.
Double double toil and trouble
Fire burn and cauldron bubble.

Camilla Bartolo (10)
St John's Catholic Primary School, Bath

Snakes

Slithering slowly
With a V-shaped hissing tongue
A scaly reptile.

Christian Preston (9)
St John's Catholic Primary School, Bath

The Lord Of The Rings

It is He that is the cause of the rustle of the tears
It is He who plays about the clouds
It is He
It is He who is blamed for a lost ship at sea
It is He who creates soft music about the woods
It is He
It is He who follows leaves to the ground
It is He
It is He.

Joshua Walker (11)
St John's Catholic Primary School, Bath

Why?

Why do cats always purr?
Why don't puppies have their fur?
Why do penguins always waddle?
Why do toddlers always toddle?
Why are buildings built so high?
Why do birds always fly?
Why are humans scared of ghosts?
Why do people like big fat roasts?

Kristian Morrison (10)
St John's Catholic Primary School, Bath

My Dog Haiku

My faithful pooch Pants,
Droopy eyes and cold wet nose,
Curls up by my toes.

Conor Sheridan (8)
St John's Catholic Primary School, Bath

Falcon

Tearing, ripping
Taking lives,
Helpless chicks
They're no more,
But in the bowels of a dark, dark cave.

Blue sheen
Beady eyes
Grabbing claws,
Curved beak
Piercing screech.

Sick pigeon
Easy prey,
Diving onto its back,
Dragging up, up, up
Then . .
Down, down, down
Splat!

Alice May (10)
St John's Catholic Primary School, Bath

Midnight Street

Hailstones hammer down
Dark black shadows tower over
From the echoing alleys
Streetlights flicker
And shimmer like a bulb running out.
The litter walks past the roadside
Pigeons flutter past
The squashed houses.
Leaves move and shuffle by.
The dark grinning faces of the night.

Joseph Marchant (11)
St John's Catholic Primary School, Bath

Risen From The Dead

I walk up to the tomb
Where Jesus lays dead
Passing the spring open flowers,
Getting nearer to the tomb.

All I can see is darkness, inside the tomb,
The birds sing joyfully,
The long brown branches with leaves lying
On the thick branches.

I walk into the darkness of the tomb
Where everything seemed to stop
I walk a little closer
Jesus is not there
He is risen from the dead.

Amy Morris (10)
St John's Catholic Primary School, Bath

Why Do Birds Fly?

Why do birds always fly?
How can their wings touch the blue sky?
Why can't the sun ever stop shining?
Why can't my sister ever stop whining?

Why do flowers have to smell?
Why do churches ring their bells?
Why doesn't my watch ever stop?
Why do birthday balloons always pop?

Why do light bulbs shine so much?
Why does my pet rabbit live in a hutch?
Why does the world have so many questions?
It must be no good for your indigestion.

Tess Henderson (10)
St John's Catholic Primary School, Bath

The Lonely One

I am alone and surrounded with rats and slimy mud
The wind blowing in my ears
Nobody to talk to, all alone
Feels like rats are keeping me hostage
Let's make sure that my life will be better than before
And make sure people have learned from their lesson.

Ryan Farrington (10)
St John's Catholic Primary School, Bath

Jesus Haiku

Angels are holy
Jesus guides us through our day
But God holds the world.

Emily Burford (8)
St John's Catholic Primary School, Bath

School Trip Haiku

Having a school trip
We're going to the mountains
Cannot wait to go.

Charlie Francis (9)
St John's Catholic Primary School, Bath

Tears Haiku

Tears fall from my eyes
Memories of dreadful times
Stuck in my small head.

Tess O'Hara (9)
St John's Catholic Primary School, Bath

Spider

S pread hairy legs on toast
P utrid glue comes out
I nk-like skin
D read of a spider coming up plug hole
E legant
R ed scary eyes.

Callum Stevenson (9)
St John's Catholic Primary School, Bath

Holidays Haiku

Holidays are good
Playing with the sand is fun
Making sandcastles.

Sophie Southcott (9)
St John's Catholic Primary School, Bath

The Beach Haiku

The hot burning sun
With the warm blue sparkling sea
The squawking seagulls.

Beatrice Moody (9)
St John's Catholic Primary School, Bath

Firework Night Haiku

Bonfires, burning flames
Fireworks are banging loud
Cold breeze is blowing.

Charlotte Dixon (9)
St John's Catholic Primary School, Bath

Hedgehogs Cinquain

Hedgehogs
Curl up in balls
They sleep when it's daytime
But at night it is the hour for
Fun play!

Olivia Coles (9)
St John's Catholic Primary School, Bath

Walking On Ice

As I walk through the scenes
Of the snow I get colder by each hour, minute, second,
But I still keep on walking as I slip and slide on the ice.

Every day, week, and month year I pray
That one day my journey will end
And when I get home
I am going to sit in front of the fire with some cocoa.

At last I could see the sunshine
Rising over the mountains.
So I followed it and it leads me to my wife on the hill.

Joshua Ayres (10)
St John's Catholic Primary School, Bath

Week Poem Cinquain

Monday
Ready to work
Children playing hopscotch
Drawing portraits on white paper
Go home.

Amy Donohue (8)
St John's Catholic Primary School, Bath

Poppy

I am just a flower surviving the spiritual
Darkness as it closes in around me.
Life is just a flicker now,
Hope abandoned, as the haunting night covers all senses.
The reek of death is like a beckoning hand
Calling for troubles, as rats scurry from death to more death,
Bringing silence as they come.

The noise begins to die,
The flicker of light begins to take a hold
And hope begins to creep through the night,
Enhancing the senses
The darkness begins to lift,
Encouraging the senses,
Back to life they come.
Signs of a new life begin to show.
Larks begin to sing,
Maybe, my life will be seen as a sign of peace.

Alex Keitch (10)
St John's Catholic Primary School, Bath

Candles Haiku

The flames are hot air
Fire is blowing in the wind
Sitting there softly.

Sam Morris (8)
St John's Catholic Primary School, Bath

The Monkey And The Lion

As the monkey and lion walked side by side
Along the once gushing river but now dried
The monkey asked, 'What makes you so grand and proud?'
'Well I'm big, smart and hairy!' the lion growled.

Hannah Phillips (10)
St John's Catholic Primary School, Bath

Raven

Black enamel paint, covering danger
Scavenges for carcasses to stay alive
Waiting for animals to fall down dead,
Killed by another
Dark as the night sky but eyes like lamps
Gleaming in the bright sunshine
Following predators through the skies,
Gliding past the trees,
Animals scurry away at the sound of its fluttering wings
Perched on a branch waiting, waiting for the cry of death
Depends on the other birds to survive in the wild
He watches from the bushes as the creatures struggle
Away from the talons of a bird lurking in the shadows.

Emer Heatley (9)
St John's Catholic Primary School, Bath

The Italian Supercar

Spitting out its diesel fumes,
Its crying W16 engine,
Breaks out 252 mph,
Only a millionaire could buy,
£700,000
Storming into the shop in 2006.
Sailing from Italy
Made by Bugatti.

Tom Prangley (11)
St John's Catholic Primary School, Bath

Winter Haiku

The days are frozen
And the cats are in the house
White snow has landed.

Amelia Morris Cuthbertson (8)
St John's Catholic Primary School, Bath

Why?

Why can't numbers just go up to ten?
Why am I not best friends with Ben?

Why are houses stiff and still?
Why do animals get turned into a meal?

Why do birds fly in the sky?
Why do people live and die?

Why do I always have to play cricket?
Why do I always get hit with a wicket?

Why do lumps of flour get stuck in a sieve?
Why is life so hard to live?

Laura King (10)
St John's Catholic Primary School, Bath

Animals

Why do birds fly in the sky?
Why do cheetahs tell a lie?
Why do dolphins jump in the sea?
Why do fish have no knees?
Why do cats always scratch?
Why do rabbit cages have a catch?
Why do hamsters like to eat?
Why do people like to bat?

Lauren Tucker (10)
St John's Catholic Primary School, Bath

The Winter's Morning Haiku

White snowflakes falling
Drifting down from the cold sky
Sticking on the world.

Daniel Malinowski (9)
St John's Catholic Primary School, Bath

Midnight Street

Blackness destroys the light as mist settles for the night.
Trees hang overhead like a bad omen of death
As balconies watch people seeing all.

Gangs hang around alleyways like bees ready to swarm
As a huge sky spotlight rings its loud bell

Electricity pylons cover the city centre
With their murky grey cobwebs
While rats scurry round searching for food.

Joseph Roberts (11)
St John's Catholic Primary School, Bath

A Great Teacher Haiku

My teacher is kind
A very helpful lady
She is very nice.

Olivia Farrington (7)
St John's Catholic Primary School, Bath

At Home Haiku

What to do today?
I know let's go in my room
I'll play cars with you.

Louis Mancini (8)
St John's Catholic Primary School, Bath

Painting Haiku

Painting a picture
Of white snow in the winter
Big snowmen with scarves.

Alessandra Di Vincenzo (8)
St John's Catholic Primary School, Bath

An Alphabet Poem
(An extract - a-n)

A is for Anna who kisses the boys
B is for Billy who plays with his toys
C is for Connor who kicks the ball
D is for Daniel who is quite tall
E is for Edward who is going out
F is for Fred who likes eating trout
G is for Georgia who is very dumb
H is for Harry who likes sucking his thumb
I is for Ian who has smelly feet
J is for Jamie who likes to have a treat
K is for Kyle who is very small
L is for Luke who likes to play pool
M is for Mike who likes eating food
N is for Nick who is very rude.

James Piercy (8)
St John's Catholic Primary School, Bath

Lonely

One day I was lonely, alone,
Full of sadness without happiness
But I saw the light, the conqueror
Of my life which made my life anew
Which died of my life to be in Earth
No one has seen this before from,
The start and to the end.

I went outside the sky was blue
The trees waving beautifully
And who made this happen?
His name is Jesus.

Talent Gwekwerere (11)
St John's Catholic Primary School, Bath

Oak Tree

You stand oak tree
As you have all of your living days
You loose your leaves then grow them again
You never change your ways
Your great thick trunk
You'd never think that once you were a seed
Indeed you were, but sun and earth
Satisfied your need
A man comes up, a sudden crack,
My friend no longer stands
I bend down and stand up,
An acorn in my hands.

Emma Scolding (9)
St John's Catholic Primary School, Bath

Fun is . . .

Fun is playing with friends
Fun is splashing in puddles
Fun is practising for things
Fun is having your favourite foods
Fun is being with your family
Fun is meeting new people
Fun is winning stuff
Fun is shopping for fashionable clothing.

Ciara Hughes (7)
St John's Catholic Primary School, Bath

Fun is . . .

Fun is playing with your friends
Fun is going out with your family
Fun is laughing at jokes
Fun is sharing with one another.

Tom Langley (8)
St John's Catholic Primary School, Bath

Alien Invasion!

Bang, fizz, argh!
Screams echo in my ears
Fire to my left, fire to my right
My leg, argh!
Ectoplasm splattered everywhere
OK we surrender
Here is your trophy
The amazing
The fantastic
Jewel of zipwangerize.

Jack Sherry (9)
St John's Catholic Primary School, Bath

Love Is

Love is a big hug
Love is a kiss
Love is a warm heart
Love is a warm-hearted family
Love is a warm house
Love is God
Love is Jesus
Love is Father Michael.

Maria Kelleher (8)
St John's Catholic Primary School, Bath

Limericks

There was a young lady from Peru
Where she played football and she drew
One day she saw
A huge paw
And that was the end of Peru.

Victoria Prangley (7)
St John's Catholic Primary School, Bath

A Box To Pray In
(Based on 'Magic Box' by Kit Wright)

I will put in my box . . .
The first gleam in a child's eyes
The first song of Christmas
A note from an angel's soft lips
The nail in Jesus' hand
A ruby ring from Heaven
An ash from a volcano
A star from the sky
My box is dressed in silver
My box is dressed in black
I shall pray in my box from day to day
in the shelter of a cave.

India Jaggon-Barrett
St John's Catholic Primary School, Bath

Fruit

F resh mother nature squeezing its way through
R ipe and fresh the seeds pour out and make a new life,
U nderneath your heart *fruit* is there.
I love the fruit juice dripping from corners of my mouth,
T rees are the producer of the lush fruit
S weet fruits grow through the summer for us.

George Cox (10)
St John's Catholic Primary School, Bath

There Was An Old Woman From Crewe

There was an old woman from Crewe
Who one day caught the flu
She stayed in bed
And there she led
So she could not go on the canoe.

Rebecca Harding (8)
St John's Catholic Primary School, Bath

The Elephant

The elephant
Goes stamp, stamp in the damp, damp puddle
The elephant
Waved his trunk, trunk and some water
Spluttered out that stunk, stunk!
The elephant
Bathed, bathed in the water
And at the same time he laughed, laughed!
The elephant had a very hairy grey, grey body
So he needed a shave, shave!
The elephant
Has a tail, tail
That was very pale, pale!
The elephant dashed, dashed
To the river to splash, splash
The elephant
Has a very fun day, day
So he went home to lay, lay in his bed, bed!

Emily Kelson (9)
St John's Catholic Primary School, Bath

The Crocodile

Snap, snap, snap goes the crocodile's mouth
He's coming down the bank
He's swimming in the murky water
He's stalking you, stalking you soon he's going to pounce.

He's caught, he's caught and he's caught his prey
Taking it underwater he's come back up
To get some more he is stalking you,
Stalking you soon he's going to pounce

He's swimming, he's swimming, he's swimming away
Swimming underwater
He's going home to his den to sleep
And to be ready to stalk again.

Ellie Bassett (9)
St John's Catholic Primary School, Bath

The Mystery Elements

There is new life on the wind's breath
Or is it the aura of the coming death
I sense the coming of new hope
For those up there who find it hard to cope
Not surprising for birds so fragile and poor
Who are roasted on fires blazing tall and wide
The rocks of earth surround the inferno's side

Now over the hills through the moor
Dive into the waves and past the bubbles
Where monsters of the deep dwell and cause troubles
Bringing down sailors and boats
Swimming in scaly coats.

Near to the sands where crustaceans and crabs
Run to picnics and steal kebabs
Which are stolen by birds up to the sky
Where we begun, and now the cycle is done . . .

Jack Chalmers (10)
St John's Catholic Primary School, Bath

Lake Of Treasures

I am a lake
A lake of hidden treasures
I hide the rainbow trout
As it flicks its tail of rainbow sparks
I hide the Koi carp
As it darts in and out of the coral
I hide the crisp packets
As they trap and kill my fish
I hide the plastic
That gets dumped over my bridge.

I am the lake.
I am the lake
That is now no more.

Eleanor Parker (10)
St John's Catholic Primary School, Bath

A, B, C Kids

A is for Abigail, who likes to cheat
B is for Barbara, who likes to eat meat
C is for Clarissa, who's as thin as a pin
D is for Daniel, who always wants to win
E is for Edward, who tries hard to spell
F is for Felix, who's not always well
G is for Gwyn, who's really quite cool.
H is for Harry, who's nobody's fool,
I is for Imogen who thinks she is best,
J is for Jack, who does well in each test
K is for Kate, who's terrified of lice
L is for Larry, who wants some pet mice
M is for Marian, who's best friends with Rose
N is for Natasha, who loves to pose
O is for Oscar, who wears a brace
P is for Paolo, who can't tie his lace
Q is for Quentin, who's friends with Kyle
R is for Rebecca, who's sailed up the Nile
S is for Steven, who wears a tie
T is for Tom, who's afraid to die.
U is for Ursula, who always wears white
V is for Vicky, who likes a quick bite!

Grace McPherson (9)
St John's Catholic Primary School, Bath

Plague Of Death

I am the death that swamped the plains
I am the beast that flew over them
Their blood they must place to stop the killing
Or the first-born son shall regret
With all of his whole life in debt.

Rowland Goodbody (11)
St John's Catholic Primary School, Bath

The City Street

The trees rustle and groan,
As the wind,
Whistles his blood-curdling tune.
Every windowpane weeps
As the rain,
Ambushes its rotting wood.
The pavement is the streets jigsaw with many pieces missing,
As the river,
Yawns in his disapproval at his numerous mouths.
The buses screech and halt in fury at every stop,
As the passengers,
Drunkly stumble out.

The clouds move across the sky in a desperate warning,
As black as death itself . . .

Stefanie Gomez-Lugue (11)
St John's Catholic Primary School, Bath

A, B, C Kids

A is for Abi whose got a boyfriend called Mark
B is for Bill who wants a toy shark
C is for Clover who has a friend called Rose
D is for Dan who sprays people with his hose
E is for Edward who stays in his house
F is for Fearne who has a pet mouse
G is for Grace who wears a brace
H is for Harry who loves a race
I is for Imogen who says she's the best
J is for Jasmine who is cool and better then the rest
K is for Kevin who is eleven
L is for Lina who is seven.

Gwyn West (9)
St John's Catholic Primary School, Bath

European Championship

E uro 2004 is about to start
U ruguay still wondering why they can't play
R aging crowds, England on the score sheet
O n and on the matches go
P ortugal we have to play!
E ngland's up 1, 2, 3.
A lmost there, give it a shot
N ow it's France who we're to play.

C hampions France have got the lead
H ow did you do it Michael Owen?
A dded time, the pressure's on
M ichael's on the ball, right now
P ulled down, down to the ground it seems
I t's a penalty
O wen's not fit to take!
N ow the penalties going to be taken by Mr Beckham
S ounds are electric
'H eh!' We've won
I t's another trophy for Brit . . . ain
P raising songs have just began!

Benedict King (9)
St John's Catholic Primary School, Bath

Football

F ree kick when you get fouled
O ffside when you get too far
O ff the field you get the ball
T all players get a header
B all goes into the goal, the crowd gets loud
A ll players are on the field and they are scared
                        but the crowd cheers them up
L eft, right, left, right as the ball goes between your feet
L iving the end of the game the crowd shouts
                      and they are happy for their team.

Matteo Sunda (10)
St John's Catholic Primary School, Bath

Names In A Mess
(Extract alphabet poem A-L)

A is for Amy who brushes her hair
B is for Billy who looks like a bear
C is for Ciara who whines all the time
D is for Derek who drinks lots of wine
E is for Ellen who is very small
F is for Freddy who kicks the ball
G is for Georgia who wears lots of rings
H is for Harry who likes flicking things
I is for India who is very silly
J is for Jill who's best friends with Milly
K is for Kerick who is a huge pain
L is for Lilly who is very tame.

Elizabeth Richardson (8)
St John's Catholic Primary School, Bath

The Plague Of Frogs

I am the frog that sprang near the Nile
That was created by Moses
I am the frog that is one of the plagues
I am the frog that hopped near the palace
I am the frog that hopped on the pharaoh's bed.

Thomas Johnson (10)
St John's Catholic Primary School, Bath

Jesus Haiku

Born in a manger
He is the light of the world
He has saved us all!

Mary Etheridge (8)
St John's Catholic Primary School, Bath

Early On A Monday Morning Cinquain

>Monday
>Clothes badly creased
>Rushing to get ready
>Running to your favourite friends
>Happy.

Hannah May (9)
St John's Catholic Primary School, Bath

My Imaginary Friend

I have an imaginary friend,
An imaginary friend
She's 10 foot tall
And she plays football
She's purple and blue
And she plays with glue
And that's my imaginary friend.

When we go to the park
We play until dark
And then we play on the swings
And pretend we have wings,
And that's my imaginary friend.

She makes me laugh
And she never baths
And that's my imaginary friend

She has black hair
And a pair of pet hares
And that's my imaginary friend.

I do my homework
Ready for the SATs
And all she does is play with a bat
And that's my imaginary friend.

Katie McCarthy (10)
St Joseph's Catholic Primary School, Fishponds

How Strange

My friend Lucy
Has a locket
She doesn't wear it round her neck
She has it in her pocket!
How strange!

My friend Claire
Wears baggy jeans
She has long hair
And she likes to eat beans!
How strange!

My friend Sam
Has a shiny ring
She loves to eat jam
And other things!
How strange!

My friend Zoe
Has a dog
Her best friend is Chloe
She goes for a jog!
How strange!

Samantha Haggett (10)
St Joseph's Catholic Primary School, Fishponds

Winter Tree

'Not at home to callers'
Says the naked tree -
Bonnet due in April -
Wishing you a good day -
My leaves start to grow as
You see them in sight -
No one understands the change in me

Can you help me?
Because I am the winter tree.

Sammi Hollis (11)
St Joseph's Catholic Primary School, Fishponds

Moon

Moon, moon you're the best
You are there with me
Moon is bright, fighting light.

You shine your light on the sky
Midnight comes dark as blue
You lead me through a haze
Calm bright
Shining light

Everyone watching you higher than you think
It brings the night to rest for day
Your moonbeam shining on us all
The sun is your friend, the stars are your best friends
You're their friend too.

I love you and I dance
I sing I wish you were here
The sun comes, I say goodbye.
I'll see you tonight!

Amy Adlard (10)
St Joseph's Catholic Primary School, Fishponds

Going To School

Hopping around
Looking for a sock
Go downstairs
To get something to eat
Out the door and on the street
Down the road I walk very fast
Hoping that I won't be last
At the gate I meet my mate,
We are both hoping that we won't be late.
Next we go into the classroom
Where the teacher's voice is booming
Now are in school at last, I'll be going home just a fast.

Terry Woodmen Smart (10)
St Joseph's Catholic Primary School, Fishponds

Tom Elvis

Tom Elvis was a timid soul
He dropped a ball down a hole,
But couldn't bear to look for it,
Since he feared the deep dark pit.

The lessons in the swimming pool,
Made Tom too scared to go to school
He really was a scared small boy,
He even feared his favourite toy!

He saw some bees,
Which made him freeze,
He screamed in his head,
And ran to his bed.

His mother came
And said, 'Oh what a shame!
You poor little chap!'
And she gave Tom a slap!

Amardeep Sahota (11)
St Joseph's Catholic Primary School, Fishponds

Godzilla

Man-eater
Grim Reaper
McDonald's beater
Rubbish swimmer
Big nose
No hair
Anywhere
Spiky tail
Egg hatcher
Eye catcher

Jordan Silk (11)
St Joseph's Catholic Primary School, Fishponds

People!

People are here, people are there,
People are everywhere!
People are different some are tall
Some are strange, and some are small.

Some are fast and some are slow
Some are small - they don't grown
People do different sports
So they wear their vest and shorts.

Some have spots and some have freckles
Some even have spectacles
People have different coloured eyes,
Some wear a wig for a disguise.

Everyone is different, even you!

Helen Smith (10)
St Joseph's Catholic Primary School, Fishponds

Help I'm Locked In My Room!

Help! I'm locked in my room!
I've battered the door with my broom
But all it did was block the lock
Help! I'm locked in my room!

Help! I'm locked in my room!
This place is so full of gloom,
It's like a castle of doom,
Help! I'm locked in my room!

Help! I'm locked in my room!
At night I sit and watch the moon
It looks like one big blue balloon,
Help! I'm locked in my room!

Georgina Ford (11)
St Joseph's Catholic Primary School, Fishponds

Midnight Sky

Midnight sky,
Way up high,
The shining moon,
It will be daylight soon,
The stars shine bright
They send off light,
In a deep black space,
Shooting stars have a race,
The moon and stars are dancing,
Some of them are prancing,
Those glistening dots,
There are lots,
The beautiful sky,
I want to go there, and I'll try,
I dream of visiting the stars,
They're even better than Mars
Then the moon goes away
The sun has come to start the day,
Will the moon come again?
Yes it will, and I know when.
When the sky turns black,
Then the night is coming back.

Alicia Chilcott (11)
St Joseph's Catholic Primary School, Fishponds

Schools

School is a blast,
It's always fast,
Work or play,
I always enjoy the day.

I like art
I like science,
I like privilege time,
And that's also,
What make's me come to school!

Emily White (10)
St Joseph's Catholic Primary School, Fishponds

War

What is the reason for war?
Who wants it?
No more war!
People dying
Families crying
No more war!
War means death
It's your final breath
War is a flaw!
Not silent
Very violent
When Blair makes his speech
It makes me shout
It makes me screech
Stop war now!

Alex McKeigue (11)
St Joseph's Catholic Primary School, Fishponds

About The Sky

Sun is high
Rockets fly across the sky
Sky is blue, deepest blue just like you
Puffy clouds all around, glowing brightly
All the time.

Stars glitter in the high bright sky
The sky is light, the sky is bright
My last wish is that every day
Everything would be bright.

The sky turned dark the stars came back
The moon shone like glitter
The darkness filled all the sky
With all the stars passing by.

Abby O'Brien (10)
St Joseph's Catholic Primary School, Fishponds

Big For 11!

I'm big for 11 years old; maybe that's why they get at me.
They point and stare and shout
What am I to do?
When I'm good they moan at me
When my friend and I are talking
They always shout at me,
Never at anyone else,
Why?
Don't they like me?
When I've done my best they always expect more
They always think they can hear my voice,
Never anyone else's
When they shout at me, I get in a strop
When I get in a strop, they wonder why
It's always five minutes on the board
Don't they ever know how I feel?
Always talking about SATs
And how we should always concentrate more, we never get a rest!
How am I to end this poem they'll probably shout at me for this!
I could go on forever on how they point and stare and shout!
Anyway I'm moving on this year!

Megan Price (11)
St Joseph's Catholic Primary School, Fishponds

The Rubber

The rubber, the rubber
What the pencil develops
The rubber erases
The rubber erases the past
The present and the future
It can erase everything!
Even you!

Daniel Cook (11)
St Joseph's Catholic Primary School, Fishponds

Bubbles

Bubbles have colours,
Pink, yellow and green,
Blow 'em around,
They're everywhere to be seen.

They're round and large,
Sometimes very small,
They burst and pop!
Maybe long or tall.

Taking its time,
To float in the air
Everyone looks,
And everyone cares.

Jordan Carey (10)
St Joseph's Catholic Primary School, Fishponds

The Beat

There once was a party on Rosy Street
There was a terrific sound of stomping feet
This is why the neighbours couldn't sleep
As the beat of their feet was very deep
They decided they would take a peep
Of where the young kids meet
And all they saw were some chimpanzees
Dancing to the thunderous beat
They decided they would leave the town
Because they didn't understand what
Went down.

Jack Kilbane (11)
St Joseph's Catholic Primary School, Fishponds

My Garden

In my garden is where I play
Five hours long
On a hot summer's day!

I'll play in my garden,
And jump really high,
Then I might sigh
Oh if only I could jump as high as the sky!

In my garden is where I play
Five hours long
On a hot summer's day!

Claire Anne O'Mahony (11)
St Joseph's Catholic Primary School, Fishponds

Homer Simpson

Big tummy,
Food yummy
Watching telly
Eating jelly
Clumsy man
Football fan
Crazy driver
He's a survivor
Strangle his son
All night long.

Yolanda Downer (10)
St Joseph's Catholic Primary School, Fishponds

My Imaginary Friend

One day when I was feeling lonely
And nobody wanted to know me
I made up a friend and started to pretend
That she was always close to me!

When we'd go to the park
We would play on trees and bark
We would play on the swings
Pretend we had wings and fly up high
In the sky!

My imaginary friend is a lot of fun
So much better then any real one!
But when it's time for tea I have to tell
Mum I have a guest with me!

My mum was up for that but wondered
Where my guest was at!
She laid out tea still wondering where my guest could be.

Mum questioned, 'Where is your friend?'
I said to mum, 'My friend is pretend but
Don't worry if you can't see her!'

When we went shopping people kept on
Stopping they thought I was weird,
Talking to myself
But my imaginary friend is full of fun
She never lets me down that's because she's . . .
Imaginary!

Almaz Larkin Williams (11)
St Joseph's Catholic Primary School, Fishponds

My Little Kitten

My little kitten loves to play with me,
She runs round the house and does a little wee,
I tell her off and away she goes,
Runs out of the room with an enormous sob.

Samantha Lee (11)
St Joseph's Catholic Primary School, Fishponds

People

Boy girl
Garden gates
Standing talking
Very late.

Mum, Dad
Garden fence
Standing yapping
Very late
Kids come
With mates
Eating cakes.

Zoe Davis (11)
St Joseph's Catholic Primary School, Fishponds

Games

Rounders, rounders
We're on the field
Scoring rounders
I want to play more.

Tennis, tennis
We like it a lot
We scored some points
And tried not to stop.

Athletics, athletics
We think its great
Running round the track
I'll beat my best mate.

Cricket, cricket
It is the best
We worked so hard
We need a rest.

Remy Chaplais (10) & Sam Taylor (11)
St Lawrence CE Primary School, Lechlade

The Dragon Treasure

It lives up in the mountain
Far above my head,
Sleeping in its deep dark cave,
Upon a cosy bed.

It breathes red-hot fire,
With scales red and green,
Teeth as sharp as knives
He looks incredibly mean.

It hides a golden treasure
Somewhere amongst the gloom,
To give him strength and power,
And keep him from his doom.

The treasure is really valuable,
It's full of precious things,
From diamonds, gold and glowing pearls
To tiny silver rings.

No one dares to climb the mountain
Nor enter in the cave,
For all are scared he would rip them to shreds
Even some of the brave.

Then the dragon strangely vanished
Leaving his treasure behind,
Along came a knight to claim the treasure
But there was a creature of a different kind!

James Russell (10)
St Lawrence CE Primary School, Lechlade

The Haunted House

Goblins running across the hall
Witches howling a ghostly call
Throughout the haunted house today
The ghouls are coming out to play
Zombies rise from encrusted graves
Dragons awoken from their deep dark caves
Throughout the haunted house today
The ghouls are coming out to play
Vampires morphing into bats
Witches flying with their evil cats
Throughout the haunted house today
The ghouls are coming out to play
Headless waiters walk around
Serving bugs from underground
Throughout the haunted house today
The ghouls are coming out to play.

Luke Hewens (10)
St Lawrence CE Primary School, Lechlade

The Dancing Ballerina

The ballerina with pointed toes,
Twirling around and around she goes,
Always leaping while she dances
Happily smiling while she prances.

The ballerina dressed in pink
Spins her skirt without a blink
Twisting and turning on the stage
Dancing with joy for her age.

The ballerina gracefully sings,
To the crowd, happiness she brings,
With a twist and a turn, she comes to a stop,
Happily bowing with a clap.

Alicia Gear (10)
St Lawrence CE Primary School, Lechlade

The Planets

The moon is a great big ball,
Made all of cheese
The sun is a ball of gas,
That makes me want to sneeze.
Earth is all green and blue
Just land and sea
Pluto is the furthest one,
Too far away from me.
Mars and Saturn are parallel
Hanging in the sky.
Jupiter seems really bare
But really really high
All the planets seem really fun
But I'm on Earth, which is the best one.

Jack Lea (11)
St Lawrence CE Primary School, Lechlade

The Fairground

At the fairground
The big wheel goes around and around
The children scream and yell
Candyfloss stands are filled with children

The water ride runs through the fair
The merry-go-round sings with joy,
The slide hung from the sky.

Coconut shyers stand by the side
Punch and Judy shows amuse all the children
Magicians pull bunnies out of the hat
All at the fairground!

Clare Hirons (11)
St Lawrence CE Primary School, Lechlade

Watch The Watch

Watch the watch and you will see
Some very interesting stuff
For example there's the second-hand
Whizzing around the cogs.

Watch the watch and you will see
A lot of catastrophe
'Cause if the batteries run right out,
You'll find it all just stops.

Watch the watch and you will see
Many complicated things
There are all the hands in succession
Now that will make you blink.

Watch the watch and you will see
Some very interesting things
The numbers round the side are ones,
To make you really think.

Watch the watch and you will see.

Simon Booth (11)
St Lawrence CE Primary School, Lechlade

I Love Summer

I love to breathe the summer air
That warming breeze blowing through my hair
To watch the bees land on the flowers,
They work so hard for hours and hours.
Butterflies dancing their colours are sweet,
And I love the birds with their lovely tweet
Yes summer is sure to find,
Our happiest feelings of every kind.

Rachael Ashard (11)
St Lawrence CE Primary School, Lechlade

My Hound

My hound is my best friend
He is black with a white chest
And loves to have a football contest
I love my hound.

He loves to play around,
When he falls asleep he is as sound as a pound
He has a big fear
Of things that he hears
I love my hound.

He loves to go up the mound,
He loves to dig around,
He always looks up at the sky,
And wouldn't hurt a fly
I love my hound.

He adores having a swim,
He loves to play with me,
And he's a dog I'd love to be
I love my dog.

Jay Goddard (11)
St Lawrence CE Primary School, Lechlade

The War

Once upon a bloody time,
We shot the Germans out of the sky
People shouting in the square
A VI rocket landed there
Adolf Hitler planning again,
To save his country in warfare.

The front line was so bloody
All we needed was the country,
D-Day was fast and quick
We didn't stand a little bit.

Patrick Docker & Ashley Bennett (10)
St Lawrence CE Primary School, Lechlade

The Film Star Fairy

The film star fairy lived once upon a time,
Never did she have the life of grime
She pranced about in her silk dresses
And she bought to match that her shimmering crown.

She auditioned for Cindy,
She auditioned for Broadway
She was in Sleeping Beauty
She worked every day.

But the best acting role
She played the best
Was in the Wizard of Oz
Forget all the rest.

She is now retired
And lives in the hills
She has a life of luxury
Including all the extra thrills.

Ellie Popp (11)
St Lawrence CE Primary School, Lechlade

Star Wars

Star Wars is my favourite thing,
The lasers all re-bound
The ships explode in the air
And fall all the way back down
Darth Maul uses a weird light sabre
I think it's called a Staff,
He has the source but the problem
Is he cuts himself in half
The Millennium Falcon's a junkyard
I'm surprised it can even fly
But when it enters hyperspace you better say goodbye
Anakin's so predictable you can tell what he's going to do
He's in the middle of a light sabre duel
And he says he needs the loo.

Thomas Jenkins (11)
St Lawrence CE Primary School, Lechlade

How Did They Get Their Driving Licence?

10 fast race drivers
Trying to get the best time
One got some chips from McDonald's
Then there was only nine.

9 fast race drivers
Not wanting to be late
One swallowed the steering wheel
Then there were only eight.

8 fast race drivers
To whom winning could be Heaven
One took a short cut off the cliff,
Then there were only seven.

7 fast race drivers
Going down a hill in a dive,
Two went down it backwards,
Then there were only five.

5 fast race drivers
With helmets shiny and new
Three had theirs on back to front
Then there were only two.

2 fast race drivers
Sweating from the sun
One was desperate for the loo,
Then there was only one.

1 fast race driver
Whose eyes were light and fair,
He farted on the sparkplug
Then the track was bare.

Oliver Codling (11)
St Lawrence CE Primary School, Lechlade

A Beautiful Sight

Look through the window,
Look through the door,
For a wonderful sight
Is waiting in store . . .

A castle gleaming
Bright and clear
Is sighted for all,
Who are watching near.

Unicorns roam
In the castle grounds,
While pretty young princesses
Try on golden crowns.

It's a young girl's dream
This world with no strife
And if they wish hard enough . . .
It could come to life!

Camilla Hewens (10)
St Lawrence CE Primary School, Lechlade

The Pop Star Fairy

The pop star fairy lived in the world of time,
Never did she spend her time in a house of slime,
She went around all the time cleaning the house,
Getting rid of all the mice,
She got dressed up for dinner and always looked nice.

When she was having dinner she always liked to let it simmer
When she went out on tour she always was in her glimmer,
She held a microphone between her thumb and finger,
As she walks around the press always like to linger.

Kimberley Bloomer (11)
St Lawrence CE Primary School, Lechlade

My Boyfriend

I was starting to become suspicious
I thought he was having an affair
'Cause he was never around when I needed him
But when he was useless, he was always there.

Once I took him to the school disco
He didn't seem to want to dance
So I screamed and shouted at him
But he just ran and I said, 'Get lost.'

He didn't come back in our car
He must've really got lost
I felt really guilty
I was so worried

I tried ringing him up
He wasn't there, so I left a message
I arranged a date to meet
He didn't turn up.

But now that I am older
I have kids and a husband too.
He was an imaginary friend,
But why did I see him at the zoo?

Amelia Tucker (10)
St Mary's CE VC Primary School, Bridport

One Day As The Raindrop Falls

Pitter-patter, pitter-patter, as the raindrops fall
The step overflows like a waterfall.

Pitter-patter, pitter-patter, as it tumbles from the sky
The thunder getting louder, the lightning lights up the sky.

Pitter-patter, pitter-patter, the grass looks like rivers.
The pathways bubble as the raindrops fall.

Pitter-patter, pitter-patter,
        the puddles tremble as the thunder rumbles.

Hannah Willoughby (9)
St Mary's CE VC Primary School, Bridport

A Horse Tale

I am a horse
My home is a stable
I walk with my owner
Whenever I am able.

We walk across fields
Road and rivers
I walk through snow
And I get the shivers.

I run in the sun
I gallop, I trot
But not for too long
I get rather hot.

I like being a horse
It really is fun
If you saw me playing
You would want to be one.

Bianca Harp (9)
St Mary's CE VC Primary School, Bridport

Claws

Claws is a cat
He is 57 years old
His claws are sharp
His paws are quick.

He sits on my bed,
He sits on my lap,
His purr is sweet,
He's near the fire at night.

Claws likes to catch fish.
He likes licking my plate,
He likes eating fruit
He is black and white.

Daniel Dew (9)
St Mary's CE VC Primary School, Bridport

Teachers

Some people think teachers
Are the most cuddliest things,
Cuddliest things.

But some people have
Different ideas
And think teachers are
The most loveliest,
Are the most loveliest things.

But some other people,
Have their own ideas,
Like teachers are the
Most bestest things,
Most bestest things.

But my ideas are
Teachers are the
Most funniest things,
Also the most cleverest things.

Like Mrs Herrera, for example
The most cuddliest thing,
Loveliest thing, the bestest thing,
Cleverest and sunniest thing
Last but not least the bossiest thing!
Ever!

Lizzy Perry (9)
St Mary's CE VC Primary School, Bridport

The Deadman!

He's here, so you'd better be scared
He's the deadman
He's the judge of judgement day
He'll bury you alive
The deadman, this is going to be the judgement day.

Jamie Riggs (9)
St Mary's CE VC Primary School, Bridport

Ruby

Ruby is my sister
She is 16,
She can be very funny,
Or very boring.

She draws and paints lovely artwork,
It's her favourite thing
An artist that's what my sister is,
She is an artist.

She never lets me on the Internet,
How annoying is that?
I know she's revising
But why does she do that?

Vanessa Thurston (9)
St Mary's CE VC Primary School, Bridport

I Love Dolphins

Dolphins, dolphins are so fun
When you look at them you
Begin to wonder how hot is the sun?
Because I love dolphins!

I like swimming with dolphins
All the time, some how I feel
I'm following the clouds
Because I love dolphins!

Dolphins have soft slimy skin
That you begin to say or sing
I love dolphins so, so much!

Ashley Lewis (9)
St Mary's CE VC Primary School, Bridport

Funny Fish

Fish like gold and silver
Darting up and down on the rusty river
Long ones, fat ones, short ones and thin ones
Crusty bank weeds all odd colours
You'll never see in your life
See the wonders of the waters
The deeper you go the more mysterious it gets
I wonder what you could see
Red, blue, purple, black and yellow
I wonder, I wonder what you could see . . .

Charlie Lawrence (9)
St Mary's CE VC Primary School, Bridport

A Rainbow

A rainbow upon the sky,
Is like a dragonfly

Shines in the sky showing all it's different colours
Which beats the prettiest flower.

Sunny but raining
The rainbows still smiling.

Now the rainbow's fading, feeling happy with the job it's done today.

Stephanie Aburrow (10)
St Mary's CE VC Primary School, Bridport

The Strange Boy

Oran is very strange,
He doesn't know much,
He says he comes from faraway,
He knows very little English.

Oran looks very different from you or I,
His eyes aren't normal,
He looks to the north,
Always.

With Oran everything's sunny,
Rain, rain, rain, tomorrow sun,
Just the person you want with you,
On a rainy day.

Tessa Summerfield (10)
St Mary's CE VC Primary School, Bridport

Life

As my soul melts, I take my last breath on this planet
Corrupted by greed and war.
As I look death in the eyes,
My heart stops beating and starts and stops once more.

As my mangled body is dragged across the ground by Death
My last thoughts on this planet,
Were of the dark points of my life.
As my life is taken away from me.

Boris Hanrahan-Lane (10)
St Mary's CE VC Primary School, Bridport

What Is A Breeze?

What is a breeze?
The breath of an angel.
When do butterflies sleep?
When flowers sing to them
What is a cloud?
Pieces of cotton wool
Why is the sky blue?
God dyed it
What makes bees buzz?
Guarding the honey.
What are cobwebs made of?
The finest silk.

Katherine Gardner (8)
St Mary's CE VA Primary School, Thornbury

Owners And Their Pets

Mr Fake had a bright green snake
Who loved to feast on lemon cake.

Mr Block who had a croc
Kept him in his smelly sock.

Young Mrs Swish has a fish
And keeps it in a golden dish.

Mr Pats favourite cat
Loves to eat rotten rats.

Lydia Rygol (8)
St Mary's CE VA Primary School, Thornbury

What Is A Breeze?

What is a breeze?
The breath of an angel.
When do butterflies sleep?
When flowers sing to them.
What is a cloud?
A fluffy ball of cotton wool.
Why is the sky blue?
Because God painted it that colour.
What makes bees buzz?
The smell of sweet honey.
What are cobwebs made of?
Sticky silver string.
What makes owls smile?
The thought of roast mouse.
What makes mice cry?
The thought of no more cheese.

Hannah Turvey (8)
St Mary's CE VA Primary School, Thornbury

Owners And Their Pets

Mr Lock had a half-tailed croc
But he only wore a yellow sock.

Mr Dat hid an overgrown cat
Who sat in a bag while eating rat.

Old Mr Jake had a six foot snake
Amazingly he had learnt to bake!

Mr Tog had a very smelly dog
Who liked jumping in the bog.

Arran Riordan (8)
St Mary's CE VA Primary School, Thornbury

Ten Naughty Children

Ten naughty children standing in a line,
One got pushed, then there were nine.

Nine naughty children running through a gate,
One fell over, then there were eight.

Eight naughty children on their way to Devon,
One saw the theme park, then there were seven.

Seven naughty children got up to many tricks,
One disappeared, then there were six.

Six naughty children looking at a hive
One buzzed off, then there were five.

Five naughty children thought they saw some straw,
One was allergic, then there were four.

Four naughty children tried to climb a tree,
One sprained their ankle, then there were three.

Three naughty children wondering what to do
One went canoeing, then there were two.

Two naughty children tried to eat a bun,
One broke their jaw, then there was one.

One naughty child having lots of fun
He had a sleep, then there were none.

Henry Wilmer & Zara Crocker (7)
St Mary's CE VA Primary School, Thornbury

The Night's Eye

The moon looms
Blooms into view
Like a flower in blossom
Waiting for the dew

The moon shines
Spines of light
Like all the stars in the sky
That always come at night

The moon gleams
Beams, a happy face
As pleased as can be
Moving at his own pace

The moon moved
Proves that he can
Like running a race
At the speed of our van

The moon goes
Knows he'll come back
Like a bird to its nest
The moon will never slack.

Ashleigh Heeps (9)
Sharpness Primary School, Berkeley

The Night's Eye

The moon rises
Cries for the sun
Like a ball of frost
That always shines

It shines like lightning
Brightening always still
Like a light bulb flickering
Like a shining pill

The moon hides
Tides of cloud
Like a white ball
Behind a black crowd

The moon's round
Sound never found
Like a silver banana
Sometimes oval, sometimes round

The moon sets
Lets the sun come up
Like a gentleman should
Now time for his sup.

Henry Knight (9)
Sharpness Primary School, Berkeley

The Night's Eye

The moon peaks
Sneaks through the silvery sky
Like a golden banana
In the sky it floats.

The moon beams
Gleams in the dark it turns
Like an orange that's grey
As it gives light it burns.

The moon flashes
Crashes its way through the clouds it goes dark
Like a person switching a light off
As the moon makes its way through like Noah's ark.

The moon is round
Its sound is never found
Like the world
The moon shape is round.

The moon sets
Sets its way down to let the sun rise
Like a falling ball only slower
Surprises the eye
Climbing down, down, down and down.

Jacob Wedgbury (9)
Sharpness Primary School, Berkeley

The Night's Eye

The moon picks itself up
Up like a human
Picking an apple up
Like a lion picking up its food
And a griffin eating its food.

The moon shines
Like a diamond
Diamonds all over it
Like a dragon called Smaug
Wearing jewels
Fools stealing
Gold.

The moon peaks
Sneaks behind a cloud
Like a mouse looking
Through a hole.

Daniel Brown (8)
Sharpness Primary School, Berkeley

The Night's Eye

The moon rises
And the stars gleam
Like a flash in the
Sky.

The moon turns
Like an orange peeling
Like a snake scaling.

The moonbeams shine
Like a star at full
Speed.

Joshua Crew (9)
Sharpness Primary School, Berkeley

The Night's Eye

The moon rises
Surprises the cosy night
Like a clear sky
In the night light

The moon flashes
Splashes in the weary night
Like a knight in shining armour
Strolling by

The moon hides
Glides in the freezing night
Like an impossible breaking ball
In the sweet night

The moon round
Curls round as it swifts in the sky
Like a sweet bouncing ball
In the night sky.

Michael Turl (8)
Sharpness Primary School, Berkeley

The Night's Eye

The moon rises
Surprise the weary sun
Like a joke waiting to jump out at someone
The night light

The moon shines
Like diamonds shining in the moonlight
Like glittery powder in the stars
And a shiny animal like the God of stars

The moon schemes
Like a thief caught
By the police.

Matthew Turl (8)
Sharpness Primary School, Berkeley

Australia

A ustralia is the home of the kangaroo,
U sually they play the didgeridoo.
S omewhere in the red centre is Ayres Rock,
T he kangaroo goes hop, hop, hop.
R olf Harris lived there,
A nd the wombat has lots of hair.
L ake Eyre has cool water,
I n Australia a Joey is a kangaroo's daughter
A ustralia is all this!

Charlotte Low (9)
Silverhill School, Winterbourne

Australia

A ustralia is an island
U luru is a big rock in the centre of Australia.
S piders are common in Australia.
T he outback is wild.
R olf Harris comes from Australia
A yers Rock is also known as Uluru
L ots of people play the didgeridoo
I t's very hot, but can rain
A very well-known place is Sydney.

Jasmine Ayres (9)
Silverhill School, Winterbourne

Sailing

Sailing in the big blue sea
Floating in the sun
Feeling the cold spray whipping against my face
The speed of the boat
Sliding neatly through the sea so blue.

Ben Mountain (11)
Silverhill School, Winterbourne

Australia

A ustralia is a very hot place to live.
U nder a rock you can find very dangerous animals.
S and is very hot and soft.
T he sand is very hot but you can burn yourself on it.
R eally blue sea is in Australia.
A and it is very hot so you would need a hat.
L ots of Aborigines live in Australia.
I n the sea are very beautiful fish and dolphins.
A nd the Aborigines play the didgeridoo.

Abbie Scott (9)
Silverhill School, Winterbourne

Australia

A borigines discovered the island of Australia,
U nder the sun is the famous Ayers Rock.
S ydney Opera House is a landmark of Australia,
T asmania is home to the shrieking Tasmanian Devil.
R ed is the sand in the desert,
A ustralia is the largest island in the world!
L ots for colourful fish swim and flip in the Great Barrier Reef,
I n Australia there are hopping kangaroos and spinning boomerangs.
A ustralia was found by Captain Cook.

Shannon Webb (8)
Silverhill School, Winterbourne

Woods Haiku

A flurry of wind
A flowing stream of water
Muddy Wellingtons.

Ella Brown (9)
Silverhill School, Winterbourne

What Is An Elamoth?

'What is an elamoth dad?'
'An elamoth is as tall as a tower
And as wide as one too
And it looks quite sour
I can tell you
Its legs are like tree trunks
Its body's like a big truck.'

'What does an elamoth do dad?'
'It browses on trees
It swims in seas
It hides in leaves
It feeds on bees
It walks on land
And it skids on sand.'

'Have you seen an elamoth dad?'
'Yes I've seen elamoths all over the world
They put me quite in a swirl
I think of them when I go to bed
They are always in my head
They come to me in my dreams
Elamoths are all around it seems.'

Perry Williams (10)
Silverhill School, Winterbourne

Australia

A yers Rock is very famous
U nder the sun rests Ayers Rock
S and reminds me of the Simpson desert
T he Great Barrier Reef attracts tourists
R eptiles remind me of snakes
A yers Rock reminds me of a big rock
L izards are cute
I ndian Ocean is on the north of Australia
A ll animals are cute or poisonous in Australia.

Cameron Nixon (9)
Silverhill School, Winterbourne

Australia

A yers Rock rises sleepily out of dry plains.
U luru is another name for Ayers Rock.
S ydney Opera House is famous
T he Great Barrier Reef is full of colourful fish
R at kangaroos live in Australia
A boriginies painted pictures and rocks
L yrebird has beautiful tail feathers
I ndian Ocean is on the north coast
A ustralia was ruled by Britain.

Nicola Bibb (8)
Silverhill School, Winterbourne

Australia

A ustralia, Australia you're very hot
U nder and along the Great Barrier Reef is not
S ydney Opera House with operas roaring inside.
T hat's when all the animals run and hide.
R ainforests and didgeridoos.
A and boomerangs too.
L arge and small plants live and die.
I n Australia how do koalas, wallabies, kangaroos survive?
A yers Rock is in the centre of them all.

Hayley Taylor (9)
Silverhill School, Winterbourne

Autumn

Autumn is orangey-red and golden.
It is the taste of roast potatoes.
Autumn is a red sunset.
It is a gigantic jumper.
I like autumn because I can play football in the leaves.

Jamie Floyd (8)
Silverhill School, Winterbourne

The Rain

I can draw on the windows
All the prettiest things
And splash all the birds on their wings!
I can pour all my energy over the town
And see all the people jumping up and down!
I can make up a rhythm by tapping on the ground
Here comes the wind who says 'That's a great sound!'
I can make the sky grey and
Gather all the clouds to make a gigantic crowd!

Kate Brown (8)
Silverhill School, Winterbourne

How's That

C ricket is a fun sport whacking the ball out of the ground
R ock solid ground so the ball can bounce and smash the wickets
I love playing cricket it's a fun sport to play
C atch the ball and *howzat!*
K it on and out onto the ground and play some cricket
E ach had a turn and had fun, it is getting near to the evening
T ime up, end of the game and the batters are all tired and they loved playing the game.

Ben Carter (9)
Silverhill School, Winterbourne

Puppies

P uppies are funny, soft and playful
U nder my bed they sleep all night
P uppy Jim is so cute it's the best ever puppy I've ever had in my life
P ut him in the bath and he gets all soapy and wet. He runs around and all the water comes flying out in my face
Y ippee he's so fun I want to play with him all day!
S o I play with him all day long.

Bryony Wintle (9)
Silverhill School, Winterbourne

Red Riding Hood All Grown Up

Skipping merrily through the wood
Who is it?
Why it's little Red Riding Hood.
But she's not so little anymore
She's got an Oxford degree in Law.
And still finds time to see Grandma
Her eyes still twinkle like two stars
But now she rides a motorbike
And climbs up mountains for a hike
Her ears are pierced, her hair is black
I'm rather surprised she's coming back
Her favourite hobby is to shop
Wearing a skirt and a sleeveless top!
She's nothing like that in the book
What has happened to Miss Riding Hood?

Emma Strangward-Pryce (11)
Silverhill School, Winterbourne

The Eagle

There's a tremendously
Big bird up there, in the sky.
It's got a huge wingspan like
A fishing rod.

Hear the superior squawk of the bird
Like an American truck's horn.
Hear the winds whistle like a chalk
Screeching on a blackboard.

Feel the air flying into your face
When the bird swoops to capture
Its prey like a marksman shooting
A pigeon from the sky

The spectacular bird is an eagle!

Tom Croucher (10)
Silverhill School, Winterbourne

Polly The Palomino

There is a horse I know
Called Polly Palomino.
In the winter snow
Her bright eyes
Glow, in the
Summer sun
We walk
And run.
In the springtime season
We love the reason
To walk, trot,
Canter and
Gallop.
In the autumn wood
We both stood
Admiring the
Breath-taking
View
And that's
Quite fine
For me
And my
Polly too.

Ellie Stephens (10)
Silverhill School, Winterbourne

Holiday

H olidays are fun!
O kay let's go in the pool.
L ook the tide is in.
I t is very hot.
D addy got burnt from the sun.
A nd I went in the sea up to my neck.
Y esterday I went to the beach.

George Mills-Gerrard (8)
Silverhill School, Winterbourne

My Odd Animals

I live on a farm not far away
And this is a story, which happened last May.
It was all very quiet not a sound could be heard
Except for a song that came from a bird.

The weather was hot so I walked to the stable
And all the animals were sat round a table.

My cow was neighing
My chicken was braying
My horse was clucking
And my cat was bucking.

I was shocked for a while
And I jumped a mile.
It was so very strange
I hoped it would change.

But that was last year
Now I'm over the fear of cooing;
My odd animals.

Annabelle Goddard (10)
Silverhill School, Winterbourne

Australia

A rea of 7,686,850 square metres.
U luru is another name for Ayers Rock.
S ydney Opera House cost millions of dollars to build.
T he Great Barrier Reef is home to colourful fish and coral reef.
R oyal Flying Doctors fly all over the country.
A yers Rock is one of the biggest rocks and there is more underground.
L ymards are animals in Australia.
I ndian Ocean is near Australia.
A borigines are native Australians.

Ben Brown (9)
Silverhill School, Winterbourne

Australia

A koala lives in Eastern Australia.
U luru is a large red rock in Australia.
S ometimes people play the didgeridoo.
T asmanian devils are carnivores.
R eptiles are scaly.
A n echidna is spiky
L ots of fish in the Great Barrier Reef.
I n Australia they use dollars.
A kookaburra is a large noisy bird.

Jodie Turner (9)
Silverhill School, Winterbourne

My Dream

Bravely I sailed down the stream
Open hearted I held onto dear life
Suddenly I saw that silver bird
That draws me forward to my destiny
For that moment I was safe
Then I went down and down to
The bottom of that waterfall
I was safe again and sailed down the stream and
That is my dream.

Tom Frost (10)
Silverhill School, Winterbourne

Haiku

A flurry of wind
Brushes through all the trees and
The autumn leaves fly.

Chloe Brown (9)
Silverhill School, Winterbourne

Colours

Red is a plump red cherry
Blue is a beautiful blue sky
White is the fluffy comfy cloud
Green is the gentle waving grass in the breeze
Brown is a cute little cat
Orange is the hot boiling sun
Silver is a lovely shining bracelet
Gold is a wonderful shiny gold ring
Violet is the evening sky
Cream is a tasty vanilla ice cream
Burgundy is a deep shiny ruby
Bronze is a bronze medal for the third place winner
Sapphire is a deep blue wonderful sky
Indigo is a beautiful stained glass window
Diamond is a beautiful crystal
Opal is a snow patch with muddy bits
Emerald is a sparkly green crystal.

Jack Williams (8)
Silverhill School, Winterbourne

Abinger Mill Pond
(Inspired by artist Edward Wilkins Waite)

The sun glistens through the morning light,
The boat that drifts gently down the stream,
The birds hover through the sunset,
In a quiet breeze.

The sound of birds calling my name,
The wind rippling along the water,
The leaves rustling along the ground.

Alone, no one keeping watch,
Safe just gazing at the stream.

Kerry Davies (11)
Silverhill School, Winterbourne

What Is?

What is green?
Your eyes are green
As green as the greenest scene.

What is blue?
The sky is blue,
Reflected in the summer dew.

What is red?
A rose is red,
Dancing in the flower bed.

What is yellow?
The sun is yellow.
And pears are yellow, rich and ripe and mellow.

What is white?
A knight is white.
A knight as white, as the darkest night.

What is black?
The moon is black.
But only black around the back.

What is orange?
Orange!
Well, an orange is orange and that's the end of that.

Sarah Bradley (10)
Silverhill School, Winterbourne

Mum

My mum looks like a pure white rose in a vase.
She feels like a fluffy, smooth, soft bunny.
She sounds like a purring cat.
She smells like a very delicate smelling rose.
My mum is wonderful, beautiful and trusting.

Olivia Stewart (8)
Silverhill School, Winterbourne

The Dolly-pop

'What is a Dolly-pop Daddy?'
'A Dolly-pop son,' said I
'Is a tall bag of peas,
Plus a girl saying please,
And a leg of a nanny goat's eye.'

'How strange is a Dolly-pop Daddy?'
'As strange as strange,' I replied.
'When the moon's in the east
It appears with the priest
Sailing out on the Dolly-pop tide.'

'What shape is a Dolly-pop Daddy?'
'The shape, my son, I'll explain
It's short round the nose,
Which never ever grows,
In the general direction of Spain.'

'Are you sure there's a Dolly-pop Daddy?'
'Am I sure my son?' said I
'Why I've seen it, not quite
On a dark sunny night
Do you think I'd tell a lie?'

Annabel Mills (10)
Silverhill School, Winterbourne

Holidays

H olidays are fun.
O n the sand.
L ying down on your sun-bed.
I am playing.
D oing some swimming.
A load of fish goes by.
Y ou watch them for a minute.
S ome boats go by and then it's time to go!

Anna-Marie Connolly (8)
Silverhill School, Winterbourne

Sunderland

The players arrive, all the defenders,
Kevin Kyle and co, all the offenders.
The streets bright up with scenes of red 'n' white,
As forty thousand people enter the Stadium of Light.
The players come out wearing warm-up suits,
Darren Byfield and Thornton with the stylish boots.
All the crowd detest the Toon,
Whilst everyone starts shouting 'Poooom'
The team go in, the tension is rising,
This is the play-off final, there will be crying.
The players are back, they join in a huddle,
The tension is mayhem, kids and mums in a cuddle.
The game is played, last minute corner,
Poom runs up and nods it in, leaves Palace poorer.
You see the skipper George McCartney
He lifts up the cup, and it falls down to the gaffer
Mick McCarthy!

Adam Hay (11)
Silverhill School, Winterbourne

Once Upon A Rhyme

Once upon a time,
There lived a little mouse.
It had a little box, for a tiny small house.

It went out every day,
To nibble some cheese away,
And then crept back to its tiny small house.

One day when he went exploring,
He saw the farm cat pawing,
And then crept back to its tiny small house.

He slept all day long,
Snoring his song
In his tiny small house.

Gabriella Chaplin (9)
Silverhill School, Winterbourne

The Best Bonfire Ever!

We sat around and made our plans
To build a bonfire - the best in the land
We gathered wood and we gathered fern
We gathered anything we thought might burn
Higher and higher our bonfire grew
As nearer and nearer Guy Fawkes night drew.

Hooray! November the 5th was here at last
All around you could already hear both whistle and blast
The night was filled with amazing colours
As fireworks were released by fathers and mothers.

Rockets soared into the air
And lit the night sky
All the colours of the rainbow
Seemed to bloom from on high.

But the best bit of all was the bonfire alight
It cackled and hissed and sent flames reaching into the night
All around people stood and stared at the fire
As it continued to burn higher and higher.

That for me is the thing I remember most
Warming my face, feeling like toast
And the teachers in my school never realised
That it was our homework that blazed in November skies!

Daniel Perry (9)
Silverhill School, Winterbourne

The Best Sport Ever

T ennis is the best sport in the universe
E nergetic, speed and strength is in the game
N othing is better than that
N ot even football
I love tennis
S o swing that racquet and hit that ball and show your opponent who's the best at the finest sport ever.

Elliott Giles (10)
Silverhill School, Winterbourne

Once Upon A Time

Once upon a time
There were three bears
Who looked quite fine,
With smooth brushed hairs.

They lived in a hole
And were very good friends,
With a soft black mole
With lots of trends.

They went to the woods
In a little red cart,
To sell their goods,
To buy fine art.

On the way there they met Goldilocks,
Who suddenly popped,
Right out of a box!
They were so shocked, they suddenly dropped!

At the end of the day
They said 'Oh no!
We've gone a long way
And we've got to go!'

Gemma Childs (10)
Silverhill School, Winterbourne

Dragons

D ragons are fierce
R aging through the town
A round they fly - burning at will
G rounding aeroplanes
O r destroying boats
N ever ceasing
S etting alight to houses.

Andrew Pagett (11)
Silverhill School, Winterbourne

The Tale Of Time

Heavy raindrops splash the ground.
The owl hoots at the mountain.
The snow starts to fall
And the tale of time begins.

Leaves grow and flower.
Lambs run with pleasure in the fields.
As the waves calm down
Spring grows.

Warmer than the sun
Heat blooms on the ground.
Fruit begins here
At the foot of summer.

The leaves glide like birds
But they fly south
And summer ends
So does the tale of time.

Peter Hodges (10)
Silverhill School, Winterbourne

The Wish List

I wish upon a time,
That I could write a rhyme,
All about fairy tales,
And following snails' trails.

I wish upon a time,
That I could write a rhyme,
All about magic wands,
And ducks swimming in the ponds.

I wish upon a time,
That I could write a rhyme,
About a car that tried to sail,
And that's how I'll end my tale.

Zak Milsom (11)
Silverhill School, Winterbourne

Belle

A girl named Belle was reading her book one day,
A beast came along and frightened her away.
Belle ran home.
She found a gun,
Belle thought, *what on earth has my father done?*
She looked in the house, she asked Gaston,
She looked in the barn . . . but her father was gone!

Belle went calling 'Papa, Maurice?'
But it was no use; she had to call the police.

The beast was running all over the town,
While Belle went looking up and down.

Belle found her father in the beast's arms,
But realised he had come to no harm.

Despite the rather frightening start,
The beast eventually stole Belle's heart!

Zoë Hughes (11)
Silverhill School, Winterbourne

Mystic Garden

One fine January morning
In December, last November
I saw a garden
Secret garden
Go away
So I entered the garden
'Are you still asleep?' said Mum
I ignored her, I shouted out
'Leave me alone this is my garden!
Go away,' I whispered.

Dan Coley (10)
Silverhill School, Winterbourne

Colours

Red is a big, juicy strawberry.
Blue is a running, rushing river.
White is a beautiful new dream.
Green is a happy, hopping grasshopper.
Brown is rotting wood.
Orange is the sun burning bright.
Silver is a shimmering, shining diamond.
Gold is a handful of shining coins.
Violet is a slithery, slimy snake.
Cream is a bowl of hot, bubbling porridge.
Burgundy is a robin's redbreast.
Bronze is the shining third award.
Sapphire is the sparkling jewels on a necklace.
Diamond is magical magic dust.
Opal is the jewel on Mum's gold necklace.
Emerald is as green as the shimmering grass.

Chelsie Sparks (0)
Silverhill School, Winterbourne

Aliens Invade

What's that?
A spaceship
Must be dreaming
Scared stiff
Mind racing
Trembling fists
Ears ringing
Eyes not blinking
Heart pounding
Cold feet
Help me
I'm going to die, *oooh no!*

Sophie Bruce (10)
Silverhill School, Winterbourne

The Three Little Pigs

Here I am the Big Bad Wolf
Come here and I'll tell you
My version of the Three Little Pigs!

I was walking to my Grampa's house when I saw,
One little pig in a house made of straw,
I said 'What are you doing there, why don't I help?'
But the little piggy-wig just squealed so loud,
I was scared a woodcutter would come
And I found that I hated the idea so I
Huffed and puffed
And blew the house down (accidentally!)
The piggy-wig-wig was killed by the fright,
And the police came along with such might.
Since I feared the worst I ran away,
Comin' 'cross another one my heart felt like a weight
Now this little piggy was cleverer,
He made his house out of sticks, harder.
Sneezing like hell the house fell down
And another piggy-wig-wig died.
The rap carries on it doesn't stop
So I'll tell you the rest in a second on the trot.
I came along past him in the street
Guess his name, guess the size of his big smelly feet. That's right!
It's the third and final piggy-wig-wig,
Now everyone just hated him
So I blew a gust and he fell right in . . .
The pond!
Splash
And died!

Mairead Connolly (11)
Silverhill School, Winterbourne

Time

Time is a wonder
Never know when it will stop
As the day goes by
Twenty-four hours lost
The days go by in their style.

Time, wonder how it works,
Who invented it?
Why do we have it?
When was it invented?
Time, oh time, you know - we don't.

Rosanna Tregear (10)
Silverhill School, Winterbourne

Jesus

J esus is in the Bible, the great Son of God.
E verlasting, never dying.
S aving everyone of us.
U sually casting miracles to help.
S aves us and the whole world.

George Williams (10)
Silverhill School, Winterbourne

Autumn

Autumn is burgundy and lime green.
It is the taste of pancakes and treacle.
Autumn is frosty mornings.
It is a warm fluffy coat.
I like autumn because the leaves crackle.

Hannah Cooke (8)
Silverhill School, Winterbourne

A Spell For Good

Take out all guns and nasty men
Add a Bible again and again
Give them soap to keep them clean
In the special world for me
Give them pets from you and me
And the insects for you and me

Round and round the cloud we go
Jumping high, jumping low

Someone's tooth of sparkling white
Someone's brain thick and smart
A school to learn
A book to work
A bit of darkness to cover people
A bit of light to make them nice

Round and round the cloud we go
Jumping high, jumping low.

Ross Lee (11)
Silverhill School, Winterbourne

Emit

Emit has two hands
Emit can be any shape or colour
Emit has lots of plans
Emit never shudders
Emit isn't human
Emit isn't an animal
Emit can be big or small
Emit is kind of monster
Emit isn't nasty
Can you guess who Emit is?
Time!

Holly Parfitt (10)
Silverhill School, Winterbourne

Mum

My mum looks like a beautiful, single red rose.
She feels like a lovely little comfy cushion.
She sounds like a greatly tuned harp.
She smells like lovely lavender perfume.
My mum is the best mum in the world.

Charles Fisher (7)
Silverhill School, Winterbourne

Great White Shark

The great white shark
Swims in the sea,
Catching its prey
To eat for tea.

It dives, dives down deep
And rises high,
And he will catch
Whatever swims by.

He sinks his teeth
Into his prey,
I wonder what he'll
Eat today?

Rebecca Andrews (10)
Southill Primary School, Weymouth

The Sun

The sun is like a yellow snooker ball
On a blue table.
Rolling around all over the place
It lights the whole world up it's so bright.
You can see it from up high to down low.
You can see the sun all around.

Elouise Langton (10)
Southill Primary School, Weymouth

Tale Of The Ocean Creatures

What brings these ocean creatures?
No, it isn't what you think.
They've just popped out for fish and chips
And a can of fizzy drink.

The creatures are a-coming.
They're running down the street.
Their bodies are a-gleaming,
And there's seaweed on their feet.

The creatures are retreating,
In spite of fizzy drinks,
Their bellies are a-rumbling,
My goodness their breath stinks!

Rhys Diplock (10)
Southill Primary School, Weymouth

I Wish I Was A Pirate

I wish I was a pirate
And didn't go to school.
I never have to learn my maths,
Or follow any rules.

I wish I was a pirate
And didn't go to school.

Chelsie Narraway-Syme (10)
Southill Primary School, Weymouth

Volcanoes

Lava
Like red-hot sparks
Sliding down the mountains
Leaping up and down like the fire
Spreading.

Samuel
Southill Primary School, Weymouth

My Kitten

My kitten is a pain in the neck
It runs around my room.
It poops on the carpet
So I take it to the market that old kitten of mine.
So I get a puppy and take it home
Then I go to work.
When I get to the house it is a mess
So I take it back to the market
After that I bought a fish and that was as good as gold.

Ross Johnson (10)
Southill Primary School, Weymouth

At The Bottom

At the bottom of my dustbin
Something's living there
But when I tell it's in it
They don't really care.

At the bottom of my dustbin
Something's living there
It dragged me in the dustbin
But I don't really care.

Michael James (9)
Southill Primary School, Weymouth

The Moon Cinquain

The moon
Shining brightly
In the sky all night long.
Sparkling all the hours tonight
Goodnight.

Matthew Owen (10)
Southill Primary School, Weymouth

Stars

Brightly sparkling in the sky
In their bed of darkness they lie
Sleeping in the day
Blue clouds in the way.

Natasha Hazell (9)
Southill Primary School, Weymouth

A Bird

A bird is like a flag,
Flapping in the breeze.

Hovering from the ground
Flying with graceful ease.

Jodie Symes (10)
Southill Primary School, Weymouth

Deadly Bats

A black cloak waiting to be worn
Like a cave full of deadly bats
Hanging from a cave waiting to
Attack!

Keeley Filmer (9)
Southill Primary School, Weymouth

The Pencil

A pencil
Is a jet flying through the air
Always ready for take-off
Never empty of fuel
But has no room to fly.

Nathan Osmond (10)
Southill Primary School, Weymouth

My Sandwich

A piece of bread
On the top
Some cheese spread
A little blob.

A bit of ham
After that
We have the pan.

A bit of butter
Will do the job
That's it
A big blob.

Charlotte Millar (10)
Southill Primary School, Weymouth

Snow

Some people say snow is clean
Some people say snow is mean,
Some people say snow is fun
Some people say we need more sun.

Trickling down as quiet as a mouse,
Little drops land on your house,
The sun will come out in the day,
And melt all the snow away.

Irina Burnet (10)
Southill Primary School, Weymouth

The Sun Cinquain

The sun
Like a fireball
Stares at the moon all day
Stays up in the sky all day long
So hot.

Emily Filmer (10)
Southill Primary School, Weymouth

The Cat Who Ate Anything

A man put a cat in his barn
To eat rodents that scampered around.
This cat was so greedy he'd eat anything
That he happened to find on the ground.

He ate smelly remains of old fish bones,
And rotten old pieces of bread.
Bulbs, flower petals and grass-seed,
And apple peel, soggy and red.

He loved to eat maggoty haggis,
And thought chicken legs tasted nice.
For this was a cat who ate anything
Except for one thing - that was mice!

Hannah Pullen (10)
Southill Primary School, Weymouth

Stars Cinquain

The stars
Shining so bright
High up in the dark sky
Like flying glitter in the air
Morning.

Olivia Walker (10)
Southill Primary School, Weymouth

The Pencil Cinquain

Pencil
Straight as a line
Jots down words on paper
Like a dart flying through the air
So smooth.

Toby Mason (9)
Southill Primary School, Weymouth

Dolphin Fever

A dolphin's my ambition,
It's all I want to see,
There couldn't be anything better,
It's just the thing for me!

Diving through the waves,
Swimming in the sea,
Hunting all together,
It's just the thing for me!

Through all the animal kingdom,
The dolphins got to be,
My overall favourite,
It's just the thing for me.

Farron Aitken (9)
Southill Primary School, Weymouth

Feelings

It hurts when people call me names,
And don't include me in their games,
When they laugh and joke about my looks,
And write notes about me in their books.

It hurts when people stare at me,
And joke about my family,
Aren't we all the same?

Nicola Sharpe (10)
Southill Primary School, Weymouth

The Sea Haiku

Falling through the sea
Trying to survive at sea,
Through the wavy water's side.

Jak Terrell (10)
Southill Primary School, Weymouth

Five Little Children

Five little children
Were knocking on a door
One broke his fist
And then there were four.

Four little children
Climbing up a tree
One fell off
And then there were three.

Three little children
Having stew
One burnt his mouth
And then there were two.

Two little children
Eating a bun
One got sick
And then there was one.

One little child
Lying in the sun
He got sunburnt
And then there were none.

Sebastian Appleby (8)
SS Peter & Paul Primary School, Redland

Father Christmas

The sun's gone down,
The moon is bright
While Father Christmas comes out at night
He looks inside to take a peep
At all the children fast asleep.
Then he decides to open the door
And scatters presents on the floor.
The moon and stars shine high in the sky.
Father Christmas says 'Goodbye, goodbye.'

Francesca Orlando (8)
SS Peter & Paul Primary School, Redland

Five Little Children

Five little children,
Breaking the law.
Along came a policeman,
And then there were four.

Four little children,
Trying to see.
One fell over the other,
And then there were three.

Three little children,
One was called Sue.
She was the odd one out,
So then there were two.

Two little children,
Playing with guns.
They shot each other,
And then there were none

Christian Holland (8)
SS Peter & Paul Primary School, Redland

Mum And Dad Are Cool!

Mums and dads are funny
Mums and dads are cool
I really like it
When they take me to the pool.
I have fun in the sun
I'm bumpy and jumpy
It's cool
But I've never ever thought to say
Thank you.
Why I've never said that I don't know
But mums and dads are cool
That I know.

Ben Murphy (8)
SS Peter & Paul Primary School, Redland

I Am A Sad Person

I am a sad person with my head on my bed.
I am a sad person crying with fear.
I am a worried person, I am lost.
I am a scared person shivering in a cave.
I am an upset person sitting on the floor.
I am an upset person staring really bored.
I am a sad person with no one to play with.
I am a worried person shivering in the night.
I am a hurt person sitting by a coffin.
I am a mad person sitting in the corner.
I am a bored person lying on the floor.

Lewis Cunningham (9)
SS Peter & Paul Primary School, Redland

The Bear

There was once a bear
Who had lots of hair
Who owned a fair
With a delicious pear.
Whatever happened he didn't care.
He had loads of fur.
He did a good roar,
He was never poor.

Adel Mebarek (7)
SS Peter & Paul Primary School, Redland

Poppies Grow . . .

Poppies grow from head to toe
They whisper in the wind
They stand on graves where soldiers die
Their stalks are as thin as thin
Poppies grow tall and lively
They face the sky, fall down and die.

Leonora Hamilton-Shield (8)
SS Peter & Paul Primary School, Redland

Five Little Children

Five little children
Standing by the door
One got hit
And then there were four.

Four little children
Climbing on a tree
One fell off
And then there were three.

Three little children
Went to the loo
One wet himself
And then there were two.

Two little children
Eating a bun
One choked
And then there was one.

One little child
Standing on his own
He went away
And then there were none.

Marino Olivieri (8)
SS Peter & Paul Primary School, Redland

The Mellow

He is as big as a mallow, and a bit yellow.
He is the colour pitch black.
He has a liking for food, and sometimes gets in a sulky mood.
He is not always cheerful.

He likes to kick a ball, but after he falls.
He is as slow as a snail, and nearly always fails.
He has got some manners but looks like a spanner.
He is as manky as a hanky that has just been blown on.
He looks like a tea-bag just been sunk in tea.

Brendan Perkins (10)
SS Peter & Paul Primary School, Redland

The Magician

There was a magician,
Who went to Japan.
He stayed there for Christmas
And conjured a plan.
He made a spell on the city of thieves,
To make sure they wash their knees!
That's not the end of this rhyme,
Because the magician made a weird sign
That makes all these words rhyme!

Ben Gompels (8)
SS Peter & Paul Primary School, Redland

The Day I Fell Down The Sewer

The day I fell down the sewer
Is a day I will never forget.
It smells like rotten fish or my dad's slippers
That he's had for seven years.
I found myself floating on a pile of cans.
I floated all the way to the sea.
I landed on a ship.
It smelt even worse than my socks
That I've been wearing for over seven years.

Noah Begbie-Crewe (8)
SS Peter & Paul Primary School, Redland

I'm An Angry Person

I am an angry person, roaring with rage
I am an annoyed person, screaming and shouting
I am a glum and grumpy person, scowling at people I see
My house is black and dark
My life seems to have a rain cloud hovering over it
This is why I am grey and my house is the only place where I sit.

Myfanwy Rothery (10)
SS Peter & Paul Primary School, Redland

Aeroplanes

The president of Spain
Drove an aeroplane while his wife
Was cleaning the drain.
His bodyguards
Mr Brown and Mr Yards
Shot him up
And he landed on Mars.
The alien on Mars
Loved to play charades
So they played
And they played
And they played
But at the end of the day
He didn't want to play
So he jumped down to Spain.

Wilf de Salis (8)
SS Peter & Paul Primary School, Redland

Sunshine, Sunshine

Sunshine, sunshine
Very hard to say
It will keep you saying
Every single day.

Rain, Spain
Very hard to say
If you keep on
Saying it
It will take all day.

Daisy, daisy dog
Very hard to say
If you keep on saying it
It will take all day.

Melanie Ginestier (8)
SS Peter & Paul Primary School, Redland

Death

I am a dark black death that causes the meaning of darkness
That falls and evil rises
For I bring fear into the hearts of good
The choices they make are the choices I hate
My creatures of misery forage for the most devastating fears
I am a devil searching for the right exact soul that I need
I am a dragon stealing the hearts of the no good
I sink fangs into the necks of hatred.

Zaid Ahsan (10)
SS Peter & Paul Primary School, Redland

The Running Of The Cheetah

I am a cheetah running through the air.
I am a boot flopping down the stairs.
I am a car seat leather and fair.

I am the colour blue, flower and chair.
I am a blue cheese, rough and rare.
I am a bluebell, waving in the air.
I am a crisp hopping with fun.

Who am I?

Marco Olivieri (10)
SS Peter & Paul Primary School, Redland

The Caterpillar

I am a green slimy snot drooling and dribbling
I am a gooseberry, hairy and green,
I am a bird, free and flying,
I am a sunflower, joyful and smiling,
I am a birthday cake, colourful and proud
I am tasty and delicious, I am a chocolate bun,
I am as shiny and as smiley as the sun.

Emmanuelle Ginestier (10)
SS Peter & Paul Primary School, Redland

Perspectives

I'm a dark cloud hovering over Dracula's coffin.
I'm a desert, dry in human perspective.
I'm a dry, hard, desolate creek quiet as death.
I'm an unused swing flying in the darkness.
I'm dead earth without a lark.

He is a bug lurking in the sun.
He is a hamster stuffing his cheeks with food.
He is a joker making even a teddy bear laugh.
He is a sumo-wrestler crushing the ball in the goal.
He is a big hot cross bun.
He is a tick bouncing in the sun.

She is a source we take for granted giving us energy.
She is a generous person sharing her skills.
She is a help always over a hot stove.
She is always there when we need her.
She saves our energy for the afternoon.
She never complains or makes a boom.

Peter Birch (10)
SS Peter & Paul Primary School, Redland

The Old Man

He is an old dog, shouting and barking,
He is a black cat, sleeps all day,
He is a lemon, sour and bitter,
He is the North Pole, too cold to say.

He is a shadow, misty and black,
He is a child, gets his own way,
He is a thunderstorm crashing and banging,
He is a rock as stiff as clay.

He is an oak tree, he stands by himself,
He is a crow, scruffy and grey,
He is the rain pounding and splashing,
He is the winter, the coldest of days.

Jessie de Salis (10)
SS Peter & Paul Primary School, Redland

Another World

I am a glass of water waiting to be drunk.
I am a little flower waving in the wind.
I am a grand piano with all my keys loose.
I am little candle lost and forbidden.
I am a small tea-bag knowing to be drowned.

I am a piece of pollen scattered on the ground.
I am a small brass pin left outside to be lost.
I am a little blanket dark and forgotten.
I am a cardboard tube being flattened by a hand.
I am a leaf as light as sand.

Martha Dooley (9)
SS Peter & Paul Primary School, Redland

I Am A Hyena

I am a hyena, I like to laugh and shout
I am a lazy frog, I like to laze about.
I am a jolly butterfly, chomping on a leaf,
I am a crazy seagull, stealing people's food.
I am a football, round, small and chubby,
I am a pepperoni pizza, eating myself,
I am a fast plane, I have amazing stealth.

Ben Mitchell (10)
SS Peter & Paul Primary School, Redland

Snow

Snow is as white as white,
It lies on the ground,
With a silent sound.
It's as cold as ice,
And it's really nice,
Snow, snow, snow, snow
It's really nice to know.

Olivia Lang (8)
SS Peter & Paul Primary School, Redland

I Am

I am a big fat rolling thing, floating in the sea.
I weigh about as much as a three ton tree!
I love to eat and that is almost all I do,
Occasionally I eat so much I turn blue.
I am always dumb and don't know anything,
Because all I can remember is what I'm eating.
I always am the same and I do not want to change,
And that is why everybody thinks I'm really strange!

Matthew Gompels (9)
SS Peter & Paul Primary School, Redland

The Sherbet Lemon

The sherbet lemon is a sticky as honey
As sweet as sweet smelling flowers
When I crunch the sherbet lemon
It sounds like a thunderstorm in a hollow cave, echoing, howling.
The sherbet lemon is as smooth as a fresh pebble out of the sea.
Sherbet lemons are my favourite Sunday treat.
I share them with my dad when we walk in Clifton
They're just so yellow as yellow as the sun and as fun as my dad.

Ceni Owen (10)
SS Peter & Paul Primary School, Redland

I Am A Dragon

I am a beating dragon flying around in pride.
Firing large flame balls from my large inside.
My scaly skin is tough enclosed in a cage
I am about to blow into a mighty rage.
I fly around the volcano wait till it blows.
Waiting for the lava to blow out the big hole.
When I hear loud thunder I blow out lightning bolts
And when the moonlight's shining beware of my revolt.

Connor Murphy (10)
SS Peter & Paul Primary School, Redland

My Best Mate

She is a sunny lemon, shining in the sun.
She is a colourful birthday cake,
Her eyes are as blue and as powerful as the sky,
Her heart is as soft as my favourite teddy bear,
You can always count on her,
She's got a shoulder you can lean on,
We are so similar, we have so much in common,
Just tell her any secrets, she won't tell a soul,
She is a fantastic friend,
That's why I hope our friendship will never end.

Sally Sterling (10)
SS Peter & Paul Primary School, Redland

I Am An Upset Person

I am an upset person slouching round the house.
I am a grumpy person sitting on the floor.
My room is dark and gloomy.
My kitchen is black and dirty.
Everybody runs away because they think I'm nasty.
My house is filled with ivy so I can't get to the door.
So I don't go out the front door anymore.

Zoe Rice (10)
SS Peter & Paul Primary School, Redland

Me

I am a crocodile lounging in the sun.
I am a hippo wallowing in the mud.
I am a sports car flying past.
I am a hyena laughing with joy.
I am the sun, bright and cheerful.
I am a field of wheat waving in the breeze.
I am a little boy pleading to watch TV.
I am an individual, me!

Edward Lang (10)
SS Peter & Paul Primary School, Redland

The Crazy Bull

That bull is crazy
It's a creepy, crazy bull.
It charged at me
When I was hanging out
My red T-shirt.
It ran away when I came with an axe.
I tried to give it an umbrella
But it got trampled on.
That's why it's a crazy bull.
I'm crazy, are you?

Sam Mason (8)
SS Peter & Paul Primary School, Redland

The Chinese Rap

Chinese rap
Nice food
Karate
Hong Kong Fuey
Very strange letters

Horse racing
Jackie Chan
Very nice dancing.

Patrick Burke (8)
SS Peter & Paul Primary School, Redland

I Am A Maniac

I am Dracula coming to suck your blood,
I am a maniac in a straightjacket.
I am a sun, yellow and bright,
I am a footballer, parading up the pitch.
I am an astronaut jumping over the moon
I am a sheep grazing on some grass
I am me who hates Maths.

Julien Harrison (9)
SS Peter & Paul Primary School, Redland

Friendship

She's a golden sun, bringing light and warmth,
She's a lolling dog, contented and relaxed,
She's a pair of headphones, calming and refreshing,
She's a shoulder to cry on, promising and trustworthy,
She's a bouncy castle, fun and exciting,
She's a forest floor, adventurous and wild,
She's a striped tiger, clever and quiet,
But not for long!
She's a lucky charm, comforting and gentle
She's a lullaby, to rock you to sleep,
She's the colour orange, bright and fresh,
She brings warmth to my heart,
I hope our friendship never will part.

Louise Caldwell (9)
SS Peter & Paul Primary School, Redland

The Sounds Of The Beach

I can hear the sea,
Crashing on the ground
It's going through my feet,
It's going round and round.

I'm a big pearly shell
Being washed away
Being swept and being pushed into a cave.

I sit down on the sand
I want to fall asleep
A heap of sand comes on me
It's just my family and me.

Ellie Craig (10)
SS Peter & Paul Primary School, Redland

The Girl

She's a bat in the corner of the classroom,
Pouncing on a book and draining all its blood,
And sitting at the back in the gloom.

She's a cat, spying on us, appearing when we don't want her there,
When she's cross she'll scratch and scream,
Then just walk on like she doesn't even care.

She's a frosty winter, sending a shiver down my spine,
Making it rain every time she goes outside,
Fretting up my voice so I can't say 'That's mine!'

She's the midnight, jet-black hair streaming down her face,
Creeping to every corner
Every small, tiny place!

Eva Mason (10)
SS Peter & Paul Primary School, Redland

I Am The Howling Wind

I am the howling wind rushing from west to east.
I am a lovely ladybird crawling on a fresh summer leaf.
I am the splashing sea with wild waves.
I am a bright bird up in the sky flying, no worries or sorrows
I am tired, goodbye, see you tomorrow.

I am the super sun, yellow bright and sunny
I am the rain, pitter-patter, dripping and dropping.
I am the winter saying goodbye autumn, it's not winter.
I am summer the king of seasons
I am always full of reasons.

Jacqueline Roy (11)
SS Peter & Paul Primary School, Redland

Who Am I?

I am a slumping cushion lying on a chair.
I am a Morris Minor standing in a lay-by.
I am a glass of water evaporating slowly.
I am a noisy flute always out of tune.
I am a tiny sugar lump melting in the sun.
I am a sponge being squished after a bath.
I am a thin elastic band snapping under weight.
I am a lonely piece of string with no friend.
Very soon I know my life will end.

Laura Vaughan (10)
SS Peter & Paul Primary School, Redland

The Pilgrim's Poem

Close your eyes look into the light
Walk the endless path through the night
Cleanse your body in the holy stream
Treat yourself and live your dream

Each step you take is a sign of faith
Deep as your soul as you embrace
Wonderful spirits rise and pray
Ready to begin a brand new day

Look into the river deep
All of the memories you can keep
Look into the beautiful stream
The wonderful God will help you live your dream

Each step you take is a sign of faith
Deep as your soul as you embrace
Wonderful spirits rose and pray
Ready to begin a brand new day.

Bethany Hopkins (10)
Steam Mills Primary School, Cinderford

A Holy Symbol

H old God's hand and be healed,
O pen your soul to the Lord's enlightenment,
L onging for your journey's end,
Y our destination is near.

S earch for the heavens,
Y our maker is here,
M emories are endless,
B uilding up your hopes,
O ver the hill tops,
L ive the journey of life.

Craig White (10)
Steam Mills Primary School, Cinderford

Pilgrimage

J ourney of your life
O ver mountain tops
U nder bridges, over hills
R ember hurry or you'll miss it
N ow it's time to rest pilgrim
E veryone bathes
Y ou've washed your soul and cleansed your heart.

Luke Haddon (10)
Steam Mills Primary School, Cinderford

Sacred

S ail through a journey of life
A ll have faith in our Saviour
C ling onto the endless paths
R eunite with your soul
E very walk you go on will bring you to a new beginning
D estiny is a way of life.

Aimee Fennell (10)
Steam Mills Primary School, Cinderford

Pilgrimage

Anxious to start the journey,
It'll be long and hard
Venturing to the Ganges
To cleanse your heart and soul.

Walking ever onwards
Many temples await
Praying to the gods
Everything will be okay.

Eternally walking towards the Maker
As your destiny unfolds
Ever drawing closer
He's almost in sight.

Years of walking the path
To see the light is the goal
The end is very near
The light is in your grasp.

Stephen Penn (11)
Steam Mills Primary School, Cinderford

Celebration

C arry the light
E verybody's glory
L eave your frustration behind
E ach step you take the closer to the light
B y the Maker of
R eligion
A nd us.
T ake your soul far away
I n the heavenly mountains
O nly you and your soul
N earest to the mountains of peace.

Jordan Niblett (10)
Steam Mills Primary School, Cinderford

Pilgrimage

A pilgrim's life is a journey.
The journey to a shrine.
Touch the holy tomb,
And his conscience will shine.

Over hills and streams,
Past forestry and trees,
Through darkened caves and ravines,
All to be a pilgrim.

Sacred is the journey,
Holy is the shrine,
Every step is closer,
To make him feel divine.

Over hills and streams,
Past forestry and trees,
Through darkened caves and ravines,
All to be a pilgrim.

The exhausted pilgrim,
Lies at the end of the road,
Pure enlightenment his,
He now has the key.

Over hills and streams,
Past forestry and trees,
Through darkened caves and ravines,
All to be a pilgrim.

Matthew Jones (11)
Steam Mills Primary School, Cinderford

Pilgrimage

F ollow the path to the endless fields of faith.
A nd find the everlasting light of the Lord our maker.
I nto a dream that you will never forget.
T ake an everlasting journey 'cross the mountains of peace,
H aving a Holy time in the rivers of joy.

Callum Marsh (11)
Steam Mills Primary School, Cinderford

Pilgrimage

P ilgrimage is a road to peace
I t's a good way to contact your God
L ife's journey takes you to extremes
G od is forever looking over you
R eligious travellers become as high as the heavens when they reach out to the kingdom of peace
I t's an amazing experience
M iddle ages is where it all began
A ged or young can do a pilgrimage
G is for God the Creator of life
E xpected to do one at least once.

Jessica Hale (10)
Steam Mills Primary School, Cinderford

Pilgrim

Journeys to a pilgrimage are special, like a child to a new toy,
Over the years pilgrims make everlasting journeys.
Unite the God Allah with all your spirit,
Religion is vital to Muslims.
Never do pilgrims lose their everlasting faith,
Yom Kippur is important to pilgrims.
Set your course on the journey to eternal life.

Wesley Davis-James (10)
Steam Mills Primary School, Cinderford

Untitled

H oly water making your body and soul clean
O ver the river Ganges cool and refreshing as we lean
L ove the God and the Lord, believe in them forever
Y oung and old dancing talking and praying all together.

Shantelle Minchin (12)
Steam Mills Primary School, Cinderford

Pilgrimage

Travelling to a faithful place.
Each stride is full of a bit more grace.
Walking with the everlasting God.
It's the life of a pilgrim, a journey to the Lord.

Finally at your spiritual destination.
Joining up with people of the nation.
Eyes closed, hands clasped together.
It's the life of a pilgrim, a journey to the Lord.

Joy Fellows (11)
Steam Mills Primary School, Cinderford

Pilgrimage

Set your soul free, like an open winged dove,
Let your journey flow, like smooth running water,
Open your mind wash away all of your sins,
Walk to the light and feel its warmth, like a moth to a
                              flickering candle,
Every eager step you take will bring you closer to the new beginning,
To make a journey of a lifetime.

Alex Powell (10)
Steam Mills Primary School, Cinderford

Pilgrimage

P leading God for His forgiveness,
I nside him is a darkened soul,
L ost it is, but it will shine,
G od will help him score his goal,
R egretting sins from the past,
I n his head, thinking of his home,
M aking his journey last.

Izzie Gazzard
Steam Mills Primary School, Cinderford

Untitled

Set your soul to the sign of light,
Like a little lost moth towards a candle lit sky.
Walk the endless path to reach God,
Close your eyes and set your feelings free.

Each step you take you'll be on your way,
The light is like a holy place.
Holy is a shrine,
It feels like you're lost in time.

Fiona Wicks (10)
Steam Mills Primary School, Cinderford

Pilgrim Journey

S acred is a journey
A journey for eternity
C an you see?
R emaining by the river bed letting his spirit free
E asily spending a life with God
D own in the deep dark desert is a pilgrimage every year.

Jack Freeman (9)
Steam Mills Primary School, Cinderford

Holy

H oly is a pilgrim's word,
O nward journey to a scared place,
L ong is the path to enlightenment
Y ou feel cleansed at the end of your journey.

Chelsea Meek (10)
Steam Mills Primary School, Cinderford

Pilgrimage

A journey for life.
Walking the everlasting path toward the Light of the Lord.
Every step gets you closer to the Kingdom of God.
Join hands with the Maker of Life.
Wash your soul, cleanse your heart and wash away your sins.
Walk day and night.
Don't rest until you're there pilgrim.

Jade Burford (11)
Steam Mills Primary School, Cinderford

Boat Of Peace

S ail on the golden sea.
H ear the Holy Lord
R ide in the boat of peace.
I n life it's a wonderful thing.
N othing capsizes the boat of peace.
E very step to the Light of the Lord.

Joseph Freeman (11)
Steam Mills Primary School, Cinderford

Pilgrimage

Holy is the hajj a time of faith and joy
Like moths towards candlelight a journey you employ.
A never-ending journey, your destination lies.
So reach out for that shining light and open up your eyes.
People from the world to celebrate this time.
Over hills and mountains to visit your holy shrine.

Olivia Pritchard (10)
Steam Mills Primary School, Cinderford

Pilgrimage

Step through the gateway to destiny.
Close your eyes, feel the touch of your God.
Be who you want to be,
Travel through life with faith in yourself.
Follow the path to the end of your tunnel.
See the light and find your soul.

Gemma Taylor (11)
Steam Mills Primary School, Cinderford

Falcon

Worm catcher
Jewellery snatcher
Air glider
Nut hider
Brilliant swooper
Paratrooper
Mouse grabber
Amazing stabber
Animal binder
Worm finder.

Kieran Powell (10)
Tatworth Primary School, Chard

Cricket

Fast runner
Good batter
Amazing catcher
Brilliant bowler
Superb fielder
Great thrower
Athletic wicket keeper.
A cricketer.

Charlie Carter (11)
Tatworth Primary School, Chard

A Rugby Player

Fast runner
Good pusher
Good catcher
Amazing kicker
Good tackler
Good winger
Amazing defender
Brilliant passer
Superb thrower
Excellent rucker
Very modest
Outstanding talented.

Joe Hare (11)
Tatworth Primary School, Chard

Raptor!

Cool jumper
Fast runner
Pack hunter
Hand clawer
Toe sawer
Body scratcher
Wild roarer
Keen smeller
Quick attacker
Raptor!

Nathan Borthwick (10)
Tatworth Primary School, Chard

Jonny Wilkinson Haiku

Jonny Wilkinson
Kicks the ball to the corner
Scores a superb try.

Nick Mouland (10)
Tatworth Primary School, Chard

Sports Day

Fast runner
High jumper

Quick skipper
Nimble hopper

Good sprinter
Far thrower

Speedy racer
Great kicker

Steady balancer
Swift dribbler

Loud cheerer
Proud carer

Tired jogger
Early sleeper.

Beth Lewis (10)
Tatworth Primary School, Chard

Bubble Car!

Volks Wagon
Wacky dragon

Blasting horn
Bubble born

CD player
MOT payer

One pink bubble car!

Kayleigh White (11)
Tatworth Primary School, Chard

Dogs

Speedy runner
Likes summer

Good barker
Out smarter

Water sipper
Chews slippers

Great footballer
Good looker

Meat eater
Good heater

Quick thinker
Slow blinker

Best biter
Great fighter
Equals one dog!
One dog.

Freddie Henry (10)
Tatworth Primary School, Chard

Jonny Wilkinson

Fast runner
Excellent pusher
Good rucker
Outstanding tackler
Amazing kicker
Superb passer
Very modest.

Henry Morgan (11)
Tatworth Primary School, Chard

Seaside

Sand between your toes,
Waves crashing all around,
Silky sun shining,
Sky like blue material,
People fishing on the rocks.

Kelly Taylor (11)
Tatworth Primary School, Chard

Limericks

There was a small child in our school,
Who did not like to play football,
He had his own go-kart,
He could take it apart,
There was a cool child in my school.

Peter Jeanes (11)
Tatworth Primary School, Chard

Football Cinquain

The best
Game in the world
With the best players like
Ronaldo, Zidane, Rivaldo
Football!

Ben Mear (10)
Tatworth Primary School, Chard

War Haiku

People killing men,
Guns are firing everywhere,
Injured and wounded.

Charles Allen-Roberts (11)
Tatworth Primary School, Chard

My Poem

There once was a young boy called Ben
Who had a little brown toy hen
He stored toys in a net
But lost them in a bet
Poor little Ben with his toy hen.

Christopher Hodder (11)
Tatworth Primary School, Chard

Summer

S mell of breakfast
U nder umbrella
M ore children playing
M aking a barbecue
E njoy cooling down
R eal summer nearly gone.

Celine Parsons (8)
Twigworth CE Primary School, Twigworth

Phoenix

It swoops down like lightning,
It swoops back up like thunder,
Then finally it quietly disappears!

Kelly de Vos (7)
Twigworth CE Primary School, Twigworth

My Pet

My pet has got no legs and it's not large.
It is as small as my little finger.
My pet has got a little tail like a rabbit but it isn't
It can swim faster than me and it's shiny and scaly like a little . . .

Sheraleen Crocker
Twigworth CE Primary School, Twigworth

Summer

S ound of the church bells
U nder the shade.
M erry sunshine, not rain
M eals like barbecues,
E verything is wonderful
R ain has gone away!

Charlotte Burrowes (7)
Twigworth CE Primary School, Twigworth

An Epitaph For Old King Cole

Here lies the body
Of Old King Cole
He rolled in his bed
And fell down a hole.

Nelson Royles
Twigworth CE Primary School, Twigworth

Spring

S eason
P ure as
R ising flowers.
I vy blooms
N ow
G loriously.

Georgia Phillips (9)
Twigworth CE Primary School, Twigworth

England International Football Haiku

England are the best!
Their football is amazing,
Pass, head, cross and score.

Jordan Watts & Oliver Brown
Twigworth CE Primary School, Twigworth

A Fantastic Fox

A sly looker
A pointed sniffer
A sharp-clawed killer
An animal growler
A furry hunter
A silent mover
A rabbit ambusher
A brave father.

Mervyn Webster (8)
Winsham Primary School, Winsham

View Of Skunk

A lethal odour
A nocturnal wanderer
A woodland dweller
A stripy looker
A tail waver
An awful smeller
A whisker twitcher
A silent creeper.

Kieran Bailey (9)
Winsham Primary School, Winsham

The Amazing Tortoise

A moving rock
A shell liver
A grass grazer
A toe watcher
A slow walker
A lettuce cruncher
An ancient crawler.

Louise Johnson (10)
Winsham Primary School, Winsham

Sight Of Bat

A night flyer
A fabulous flapper
An insect attacker
A people screamer
A silent waiter
A church nester
An echo user
A poky predator.

Samuel Harris (9)
Winsham Primary School, Winsham

The Prickly Hedgehog

A spiky football
A bramblely feeler
A warm thinker
A night-time feeder
A frightened creature
A black-nosed looker
A quiet mover.

Michael Pugh (9)
Winsham Primary School, Winsham

A Fox's View

A devious creature
A clever teacher
A cautious liver
A graceful runner
A merciless killer.

Benjamin Harris (11)
Winsham Primary School, Winsham

Sight Of Fox

A white-tipped brush
A sly stepper
A rabbit hunter
A lightning swerver
A chicken gobbler
A viscious fighter
A haunted killer.

Billie-Ann Warren (11)
Winsham Primary School, Winsham

The Snapping Hyena

A fast attacker
A fierce laugher
A bone cruncher
A sneaky thiever
A spotty mover
A savannah liver
An animal diner.

Cain Davies (8)
Winsham Primary School, Winsham

Black Leopard Panther

A black shadow
A night hunter
A sleek creeper
A good mother
An animal muncher
An easy pacer
A lightning mover.

Adrian Shakespeare (9)
Winsham Primary School, Winsham

Sweet Little Budgie

A seed nibbler
A rainbow flapper
A whistling singer
A helicopter twirler
A mirror watcher
A perch stander
A sneaky mimicker
A clever trickster.

Kirsty Love (9)
Winsham Primary School, Winsham

The Cuddly Cat

A fast runner
A mouse hunter
A puddle drinker
A silent predator
A quick thinker
A furniture scratcher
A comforting miaower
A night-time wanderer.

Scott Curtis (10)
Winsham Primary School, Winsham